THE OFFICIAL **NATIONAL PARK GUIDE**

PEMBROKESHIRE COAST

Text by Alf Alderson · Photographs by John Cleare

SERIES EDITOR **Roly Smith**

PEVENSEY GUIDES

The Pevensey Press is an imprint of
David & Charles

First published in the UK in 2001

Map artwork by Chartwell Illustrators
based on material supplied by the
Pembrokeshire Coast National Park
Authority

A catalogue record for this book is
available from the British Library.

ISBN 1 898630 14 3

Book design by Les Dominey Design
Company, Exeter
and printed in Hong Kong by
Hong Kong Graphics and
Printing Ltd
for David & Charles
Brunel House Newton Abbot Devon

Contents

Page 1: Manorbier Bay: rising tide on the little beach below the castle. East Moor Cliff in the distance
Pages 2 and 3: On the Pembrokeshire Coast Path: young hikers descend the Gribin Ridge above Solva harbour
Left: Bosherston: view northward up the eastern lily pool towards the classic eight-arched bridge, one of the few remaining features of the old Stackpole Court estate (now National Trust)
Front cover: (above) Looking over Porth Mynawyd to the craggy headland of Dinas Fach from the Pembrokeshire Coast Path; (below) Tenby: the colourful Regency houses of St Julian's Terrace above the harbour; (front flap) the tiny harbour of Porth Clais near St David's
Back cover: Looking up the wild western coast of the Strumble peninsula from above Pwll Deri

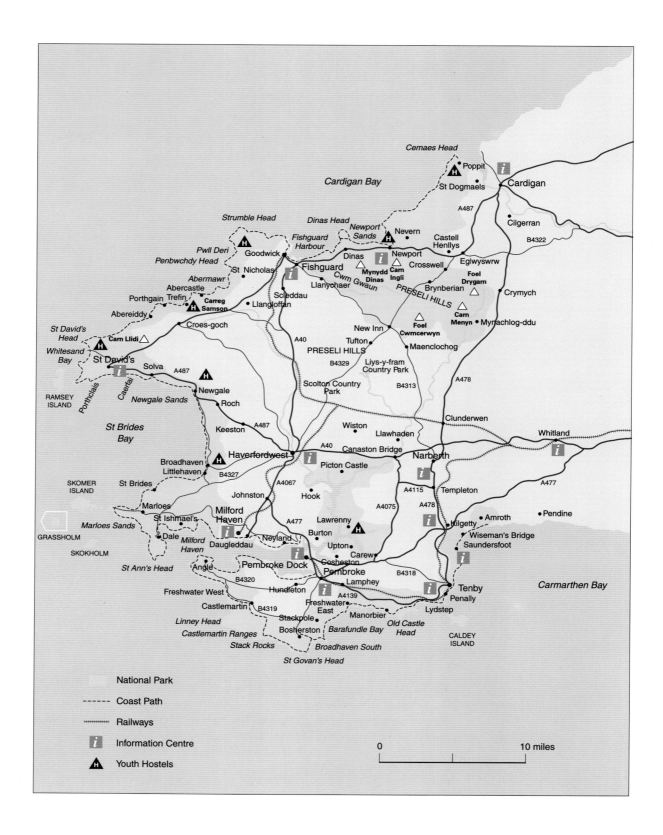

National Park

------- Coast Path

++++++++ Railways

i Information Centre

H Youth Hostels

0   10 miles

Foreword

by Professor Ian Mercer CBE, Secretary General, Association of National Park Authorities

The National Parks of Great Britain are very special places. Their landscapes include the most remote and dramatic hills and coasts in England and Wales, as well as the wild wetlands of the Broads. They still support the farming communities which have fashioned their detail over the centuries. They form the highest rank of the protected areas which society put in place in 1949. So, 1999 saw the fiftieth anniversary of the founding legislation which, incidentally, provided for Areas of Outstanding Natural Beauty, Nature Reserves, Areas of Special Scientific Interest and Long Distance Footpaths, as well as for National Parks.

In the eight years following that, ten Parks were designated. The Lake District, the Peak, Snowdonia and Dartmoor were already well visited, as were the North York Moors, Pembrokeshire Coast, Yorkshire Dales and Exmoor which quickly followed. The Brecon Beacons and Northumberland had their devotees too, though perhaps in lesser numbers then. The special quality of each of these places was already well known, and while those involved may not have predicted the numbers, mobility or aspirations of visitors accurately, the foresight of the landscape protection system cannot be too highly praised.

That system has had to evolve – not just to accommodate visitor numbers, but to meet the pressures flowing from agricultural change, hunger for housing and roadstone, thirst for water, and military manoeuvring – and indeed, the Norfolk and Suffolk Broads were added to the list in 1989. National Parks are now cared for by free-standing authorities who control development, hold land, grant-aid farmers and others, provide wardens, information, car parks and loos, clear footpaths and litter, plant trees and partner many other agents in pursuit of the purposes for which National Parks exist. Those purposes are paramount for all public agencies' consideration when they act within the Parks. They are:

- the conservation of the natural beauty, wildlife and cultural heritage of the area, and
- the promotion of the understanding and enjoyment of its special qualities by the public.

The National Park Authorities must, in pursuing those purposes, foster social and economic well-being. They now bring in some £48 million a year between them to be deployed in the Parks, in addition to normal local public spending.

This book is first a celebration of the National Park, of all its special qualities and of the people whose predecessors produced and maintained the detail of its character. The series to which this book belongs celebrates too the first fifty years of National Park protection in the United Kingdom, the foresight of the founding fathers, and the contributions since of individuals like John Sandford, Reg Hookway and Ron Edwards. The book and the series also mark the work of the present National Park Authorities and their staff, at the beginning of the next fifty years, and of the third millennium of historic time. Their dedication to their Parks is only matched by their aspiration for the sustainable enhancement of the living landscapes for which they are responsible. They need, and hope for, your support.

In the new century, national assets will only be properly maintained if the national will to conserve them is made manifest to national governments. I hope this book will whet your appetite for the National Park, or help you get more from your visit, and provoke you to use your democratic influence on its behalf. In any case it will remind you of the glories of one of the jewels in Britain's landscape crown. Do enjoy it.

Introducing the Pembrokeshire Coast

Pembrokeshire ... remains a separate, unique and astonishingly beautiful county ...

Wynford Vaughan Thomas, *A Pembrokeshire Anthology*, 1982

The Pembrokeshire Coast National Park is the only predominantly coastal National Park in Britain. Soaring cliffs, long golden beaches, hidden coves and harbours, wide, open estuaries and wind-whipped dunes make up a coastal landscape that is among the most beautiful in Europe, while offshore are a range of islands of international importance as wildlife habitats.

Inland the rolling Preseli Hills rise up to almost 2,000ft (600m) above the Irish Sea, while beneath them the wooded seclusion of the Gwaun Valley has seen little change as the twentieth century has come and gone, and the Daugleddau Estuary is a haven of peace and quiet for humans and wildlife alike.

As long ago as the eleventh century the Celts were referring to Pembrokeshire as 'the land of mystery and enchantment' (*gwlad hud a lledrith*) in *The Mabinogion*, a classic collection of medieval folk tales, and in 1188, Giraldus Cambrensis of Manorbier wrote that 'Penbroch' was '...the finest part' of '...the most beautiful' area of Wales. Eight centuries later millions of visitors come every year to discover exactly what he meant.

Well before Giraldus, Pembrokeshire had established itself as a unique corner of the British Isles. The inspiring scenery, the sparkling light for which modern-day artists and photographers value the area, and the spiritual qualities of the landscape have probably been recognised since prehistoric times.

Left: Skomer: on the island's northern cliffs above the Garland Stone

Above: Detail of an ancient cliff-top wall

The Preseli Hills and coastal promontories such as Strumble Head were the favoured sites for early settlements. The inhabitants left their mark on the landscape in various ways, from megalithic stones, like the King's Quoit alongside the coast path at Manorbier, to the ramparts of earth and stones which make up the defensive walls of an Iron Age settlement such as that at St David's Head. Particularly impressive relics of these distant days are to be seen at Carreg Samson near Abercastle, and Pentre Ifan in the foothills of the Preselis, but you have to travel to Salisbury Plain in England to see what is perhaps Pembrokeshire's most enduring prehistoric monument, in the form of the bluestones which make up the inner horseshoe of Stonehenge.

Below: The remote little church at Glanduad near the Castell Henllys Iron Age site

No one knows for sure just how or why eight individual stones weighing as much as four tons were transported all that distance. Some claim they are glacial erratics, others that it was through human labour and ingenuity, and if the latter theory is correct, it says a lot for the way in which Pembrokeshire was regarded in spiritual terms by early residents of Britain.

Indeed, spirituality continued to be a prime feature of life in Pembrokeshire into the Dark Ages. Early saints must have been bumping into each other *en route* to their hermit's cells in the fifth and sixth centuries – a period known locally as the Age of Saints – and many myths and

legends surround their activities. The most famous of all is, of course, Wales's patron saint, St David (*Dewi Sant*), who is reputed to have established a monastery where St David's Cathedral stands today. The settlement that bears his name today is officially Britain's smallest city.

The cathedral, in fact, became Pembrokeshire's first 'visitor attraction'. In the Middle Ages, the Church declared that two pilgrimages to St David's Cathedral were the equal of one to Rome. This in itself says something about the inaccessibility of this corner of Britain at that time, and even though the Normans invaded Pembrokeshire in the late eleventh century, the culture and traditions of the original Celtic inhabitants were far from overwhelmed, particularly in the north of the county.

The Norman stronghold was in the south, with Pembroke Castle being the most obvious example of this. To the north-west the native Welsh people and their culture remained strong. A dividing line of castles running through Llansteffan, Laugharne, Narberth, Llawhaden, Wiston, Haverfordwest and Roch, above St Bride's Bay, separated the two cultures, and this divide was marked by the imaginary 'Landsker Line', derived from a Norse word meaning frontier. Even today the Landsker separates the 'Englishry' of 'Little England beyond Wales' from the 'Welshry' to the north-west, where the Welsh language and traditional Welsh customs are much more evident.

The use of the Norse word 'Landsker' also indicates the influence of the Vikings on the area. Between the ninth and eleventh centuries they periodically raided Pembrokeshire and left their mark in various place names, most notably the islands of Skomer, Skokholm, Grassholm and Ramsey.

Throughout the Middle Ages, other than providing England and Wales with

Above: At the base of so-called Dinas Island is the tranquil cove of Cwm-yr-Eglwys. The view is eastward to the headlands beyond Newport Bay

Above: The bizarre pinnacle of
Maiden Castle is one of several such
crags that rise over the Treffgarne
Gorge near Wolf's Castle; the Preseli
Hills line the horizon

the Tudor dynasty, Pembrokeshire's influence on life in Britain was relatively small
– it was, after all, a long way off the beaten track. Coastal traders would stop off at
ports and harbours such as Tenby, Angle, Dale, Haverfordwest, Solva and
Newport, which sprang up to service the increasing traffic along the Bristol
Channel and across to Ireland and western Europe. Industrial development came
in the form of relatively small-scale coal mining around Saundersfoot, the
Daugleddau and the southern end of St Bride's Bay, iron working at Stepaside and
slate quarrying in north Pembrokeshire, but it was not really until the Industrial
Revolution that visitors and travellers began to arrive in Pembrokeshire in any sig-
nificant numbers.

This was due to the development of the railways in the mid-nineteenth century,
which saw the Great Western Railway extending west into Pembrokeshire, and the
opening up of the ports of Fishguard, Milford Haven, Neyland and Pembroke
Dock, which was the site of the Royal Naval Dockyard from 1814-1926. Along
with this came the arrival of the first tourists, mainly to Tenby.

It was here that Victorian visitors took to the waters in bathing carriages, lis-
tened to music beside the bandstand, and enjoyed the bracing walks and sea views
for which Pembrokeshire later became famous. But tourism was slow to grow and
remained very much the preserve of the well-heeled for many decades. It was only
after World War II that tourism began to take over from agriculture and fishing as
Pembrokeshire's main source of income, especially as car ownership increased and
road access to the area improved.

However, well before the tourist boom some early visitors and inhabitants of
Pembrokeshire were well aware of its importance and attraction as both a wildlife
habitat and as a place of unforgettable landscapes – the naturalist R.M. Lockley,

for example, set up the first bird observatory in Britain on Skokholm in 1933, while the painter Graham Sutherland was inspired to produce many of his best works by the Pembrokeshire landscape.

In the second half of the twentieth century new industries developed in Pembrokeshire, in particular around the Milford Haven waterway, once described by Lord Nelson as the world's finest deepwater harbour, and eulogised by Shakespeare:

> *... how far it is*
> *to this same blessed Milford; and, by the way,*
> *Tell me how Wales was made so happy as*
> *To inherit such a haven.*
> Imogen in *Cymbeline*, Act III, scene 2

Since the county's first oil refinery was built here in 1950 and the various towers and chimneys of the refinery and the nearby Pembroke Power Station (now scheduled for demolition) can be seen from much of Pembrokeshire, Shakespeare might not have quite the same view were he writing today. This kind of development is not what you might expect in and beside a National Park, and has long been a contentious issue, but it remains important to the local economy for the employment opportunities it offers.

The worst imaginable scenario – and the one which environmentalists had long worried about – occurred in February 1996 when the oil tanker *Sea Empress* ran

Pages 14-15: June on Skomer: view eastwards over South Haven towards The Neck peninsula and the mainland beyond
Below: Sailing through the treacherous Ramsey Sound - running close inshore to avoid The Bitches. Ramsey farmhouse stands on the cliff-top

Above: View along the cliff-top above Pwll Deri towards Penbwchdy Head; on the left the coast stretches away towards Abercastle

aground just outside the waterway, spilling 72,000 tonnes of oil. The environment eventually recovered, but this incident emphasised the often conflicting uses of National Parks which occur throughout England and Wales. The very beauty that gives the area National Park status can also be an important economic asset which may easily conflict with the aims of the National Park Authority.

For most visitors, however, such apparent anachronisms are easily lost in a landscape as magnificent as Pembrokeshire's, and it was this landscape and its wildlife which led to the area being designated a National Park in 1952. Then, Pembrokeshire was a very remote corner of Britain – the author Norman Lewis, staying in a cottage in Little Haven around this time, describes how his accommodation had no running water, no sanitary facilities and no electricity. Things are rather different today, of course, yet despite the fact that Pembrokeshire is relatively easy to get to now, it's still a long way from the hassles of twenty-first century life.

This is one of Britain's smallest National Parks, yet it's the most densely populated, with around 24,500 permanent residents. Nowhere in the Park is more than 10 miles (16km) from the sea and most places are within 2 miles (3km) of it. There are some 50 beaches, a 186-mile (299km) National Trail along the coast, and inland hills, valleys and river estuaries among which it is still quite possible to relax

and unwind, away from the pressures of urban living.

The coastline is a place of superlatives. Pembrokeshire's islands beckon from across flowing tidal races, promising excitement and discovery, and all the major islands can be visited by boat in summer. The waters around Skomer make up one of only two Marine Nature Reserves in Britain, and together with nearby Skokholm and Middleholm islands, Skomer shares the world's largest population of Manx shearwaters. Grassholm Island, 7 miles (11km) out to sea, has the fourth largest gannetry in the world, and Ramsey Island, Skomer and the mainland support the largest grey seal colony in southern Britain.

In early summer you can enjoy gloriously colourful displays of wildflowers along the coast path; year-round you may see seals and porpoises diving through clear green waters; and in the winter months you can watch in awe as 65ft (20m) high headlands disappear beneath the sea spray in spectacular gales.

This same coastline is becoming an increasingly popular playground; from Coast Path walkers to climbers, surfers to divers, bathers to sandcastle builders, this is an area that – in summer especially – can pretty much provide an activity to suit anyone.

With such a superb coastline, it's easy to forget about the hills and valleys which comprise a large and equally important part of the National Park. From the rolling

blue Preseli Hills you can enjoy some of the best views in all Wales, and the sense of their prehistoric past almost hangs in the air. Standing stones such as the impressive megalith of Pentre Ifan, and summits like Foel Drygarn with its Iron Age remains, give these hills a special atmosphere. The past also lingers on in the beautiful Gwaun Valley, hidden beneath the Preselis, where little has changed the landscape over the centuries, other than a metalled road and a few telephone lines. Welsh language and culture is strong in this hidden corner of the National Park, and wildlife such as otters, herons, foxes and badgers find this an ideal habitat.

The Daugleddau – the upper reaches of the Milford Haven waterway, splitting as it does into the Eastern and Western Cleddau – also tends to be overlooked in the rush for the coast. The Western Cleddau's source is near Croesgoch, the Eastern Cleddau flows from the Preseli Hills, and the two meet at Picton Point, where they flow into the wide and tranquil waters of the Milford Haven estuary.

This is another wildlife haven, rich in birdlife, especially waders and migratory visitors, and the pastoral landscape of the area makes it a great place to relax, whether walking the riverbanks or boating. The small settlements along the riverbanks have a rich history, from the impressive bulk of Carew Castle, now leased by the National Park Authority, to small communities such as Landshipping, where coal was once exported from local pits, or further upstream Slebech, a Commandery of the Knights Hospitallers of the Order of St John in the twelfth century.

The huge variety and sheer beauty of this landscape are prime reasons for its designation as a National Park. And as more and more people come to realise just how much the Pembrokeshire coast has to offer, the landscape and environment come under ever-increasing pressure from both the numbers of visitors and the necessity of providing facilities for them. Add to that the need to develop the area so that local people can enjoy a decent quality of life and you can see that maintaining the present landscape and beauty of the National Park while moving forward into the new millennium is a tricky balancing act.

The National Park Authority in its current format came into being in 1996 after local government reorganisation, although the Authority has been around since February 1952, after being created under the provisions of the National Parks and Access to the Countryside Act 1949.

The primary role of the Authority is to:

- conserve the natural beauty, wildlife and cultural heritage of Pembrokeshire;
- promote opportunities for enjoyment and understanding of the special qualities of the National Park;
- foster the well-being of the local community.

To do this, the Authority employs 100 full-time staff and some 30 seasonal staff, while valuable work is also done by around 70 voluntary wardens.

The Pembrokeshire Coast National Park covers an area of 240 square miles (620sq km), and has within it 260 miles (418km) of coastline. There are 75 Sites of Special Scientific Interest (SSSIs), 6 National Nature Reserves, 1 Marine Nature Reserve, 7 Special Areas of Conservation and 4 Special Protection Areas.

In addition the Park has 257 Scheduled Ancient Monuments, 12 Conservation Areas, 1,038 Listed Buildings and 478 miles (769km) of Public Rights of Way, plus 186 miles (299km) of Coast Path to look after.

That's an awful lot of facts and figures to digest, but what it basically comes down to is a great deal of important conservation and development work for the National Park Authority.

Not all the work is done by the Authority on its own, however. Organisations such as the National Trust, the Wildlife Trust West Wales, the RSPB and the Forestry Authority own large areas of land in the Park and work alongside the Authority to ensure it is used appropriately. Indeed, the National Park Authority owns only 2 per cent of the land within the National Park, the rest belonging to private landowners – in fact none of the National Parks in England and Wales are owned by the nation, despite their name. This means working carefully with landowners to ensure the Park provides adequately for all - residents, visitors and wildlife.

This is a thought worth bearing in mind the next time you enjoy a stroll along the Pembrokeshire Coast Path. After all, however natural it may look, it wouldn't necessarily be there without the work of the National Park Authority.

Opposite: A summer sunset over the North Bishop skerries
Below: The Coast Path descends towards the deep inlet of Pwll Deri en route to Penbwchdy Head (left); Dinas Mawr with its earthworks on the right

1 The rocks beneath: geology and scenery

Opposite: This magnificent example of an anticline occurs among the folded strata in Pwllcrochan, a difficult-to-reach cove on the Strumble peninsula
Below: The steep cliffs above Pwll Deri are well known to rock climbers

Stones, the sea and the weather have moulded the look of Pembrokeshire. Man has merely scratched its surface.

Vyvyan Rees, *South West Wales*, 1963

The Pembrokeshire Coast National Park contains more variety of geological features than virtually anywhere else in Britain, with rocks ranging in age from some of the very oldest (the 600 million-year-old Precambrian granophyre of Porth Clais) to some of the youngest, in the form of 3,000-year-old cemented dune sands.

Earth movements such as folding and faulting have affected the area over aeons, while in more recent geological time the landscape has been shaped by the action of the Irish Sea ice sheet some 18,000 years ago and frost, rain, sun, wind and sea up to the present day. This has affected everything from the frost-shattered crags of the Preseli Hills to the wave-battered cliffs and bays of the coastline.

As you walk the coastline you can see many features that would normally be hidden from view, as the cliffs provide a cross-section of the rocks beneath your feet. Travelling across the higher ground of the Preseli Hills also allows you to see the geographical layout of the entire Park, providing a unique feel for the landscape.

COASTAL FEATURES

It may seem a bit obvious that any stretch of coastline would consist of a series of cliffs and bays, but how were they formed? Sea cliffs, highest between Pen-yr-Afr and Cemaes Head on the north coast, at 550ft (168m), are formed as a direct result of erosion by the sea, especially during severe storms – and few stretches of Pembrokeshire's coastline are not regularly hit by gales.

It's not just the wind and waves that do the damage – driftwood, pebbles and even boulders may be picked up by the sea and flung ashore, and when this material is dashed against the base of the cliff, it can cause erosion, undercutting and the eventual collapse of the strata above into the sea. As the land retreats, on occasion the Coast Path and valuable farmland can be lost to the ocean. You can see a good example of this above

Above: The wall of limestone cliffs at Proud Giltar, north of Lydstep Haven, rises nearly 150ft (45m) above the waves

Abermawr beach, where the original line of the Coast Path now hangs out into empty space.

The material which lands at the foot of the cliff as a result of this battering by the elements may provide some protection from further erosion, but only for the relatively short period before it is washed away by the waves.

As the cliff recedes it leaves a gently sloping, irregular 'wave-cut platform' at its base, and although common around the coast there are particularly good examples between Amroth and Saundersfoot and at the south end of Freshwater West.

Obviously the weaker the rocks of a cliff, the more quickly it will erode, so that 'soft' rocks, such as the 300-million-year-old Carboniferous shales and sandstones of St Bride's Bay, have eroded more rapidly than 'hard' rocks, like the 470-million-year-old Ordovician gabbro of St David's Head. Also, very old rocks tend to be more resistant than younger ones, although this is only a broad generalisation.

The peninsulas that you see - such as the Marloes Peninsula - are composed of harder, more resistant rocks than the bays which lie inside them. The islands lying off the coast are also made up of harder, resistant rocks and thus still stand proud above the waves. Skomer, for instance, is composed mainly of Silurian volcanic lavas and tuffs which date back some 435 million years.

This pattern of alternating headlands and bays is repeated on a smaller scale all along the coast, so that wherever you have a bay or cove you know that the rocks are weaker here than the headlands on either side. Examples include Lydstep Haven in south Pembrokeshire, where a sequence of weak Carboniferous sandstones and shales – further weakened by a fold in the rocks – is bounded on either side by the more resistant Carboniferous limestone of Giltar Point and Lydstep Point; and bays such as Abereiddi, between the hard igneous headland of St David's

Head and Strumble Head, which is made up of easily eroded Ordovician slates.

Some of the most dramatic coastal features in Britain occur around the Pembrokeshire coast, especially off the Carboniferous limestone cliffs of the Castlemartin area. Although the stacks, caves, blowholes and arches to be found between St Govan's Head and Linney Head are not unique within the National Park, they are at their most spectacular here. This is largely due to the fact that Carboniferous limestone is soluble in water, leading to impressive erosive effects.

Several of the sea caves of the Castlemartin area have been formed by the action of sea, rain and ground water on joints and bedding planes within the rock, eroding and opening these out over time to form cavities. Sea caves are also common elsewhere along the coast. In some cases they may have been formed by the erosion of weak rocks beneath more resistant strata, such as Fox Hole at Little Haven; in other instances the sea may have been able to erode along a weakness in the rock such as a fault line.

Blowholes form after partial collapse of a cave roof, resulting in a 'chimney' connecting the base of the cave with the cliff top. In stormy conditions the sea can rush into the cave and blast up through the chimney to produce an impressive spume of water. Blowholes are quite common along the cliffs between Linney Head and St Govan's Head, although some are reworked limestone features rather than 'pure' blowholes as described above. Another interesting feature along this stretch of coastline is the narrow inlet of Huntsman's Leap near St Govan's Head. It is the result of erosion along a fault line.

Above: Characteristic limestone features at Skrinkle Haven between Manorbier and Lydstep; on the left the white limestone gives way to red sandstone
Below: The vertical limestone crags of St Govan's Head have become a rock climbers' playground

Above & right: Celebrated features on the Castlemartin coast: the Green Bridge of Wales and the nearby Elegug Stacks, first climbed in 1970

Arches can occasionally be seen along the more exposed areas of the Pembrokeshire coast, and the best-known example is the Green Bridge of Wales near Flimston. This was formed by the retreat of the coastline into an area of heavily eroded and weathered karst (limestone) scenery. Other arches, such as Den's Door near Broad Haven, are formed by two caves on opposite sides of a headland uniting to form one large hole in the rock. There are also good examples of an arch and a blowhole just south of Ceibwr Bay at The Witches' Cauldron.

Stacks are often the remnants of collapsed arches - although they can also occur as a result of well-jointed surrounding strata being eroded around them. Stacks are common along many more exposed areas the Pembrokeshire coast. The best-known examples are Elegug Stacks near Flimston, but there is also easy access to an example at Porth Lleuog, just north of Whitesands Bay.

Right: Dramatically coloured cliffs on the Old Red Sandstone of the Angle peninsula's southern coast
Opposite: The wide sands at Newgale are fully exposed only at low tide; the upper beach is known for its pebbles
Pages 26-7: Low tide on the fine sands of Traeth Llyfn near Aber Eiddy

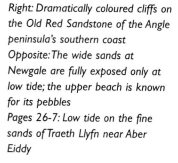

FOLDING AND FAULTING

One of the great features of walking along the Coast Path is that in many places you can literally see inside the earth, for where sea cliffs are exposed it's as if someone had cut through a section of the earth's crust to reveal the inner structure. The effects of folding and faulting are especially well seen in these circumstances.

Both are associated with earth movements. In the geological past many of the area's rocks were subjected to intense earth movements, known as orogenies, over periods of several million years. The folding now seen in Pembrokeshire was caused by relatively localised plate collisions occurring during the Caledonian Orogeny, 400 million years ago, and the Variscan Orogeny 290 million years ago. Both of these folded, twisted, and fractured rocks within Pembrokeshire.

Examples of folding can be seen at various spots along the coast. At Poppit you can see small synclines (downfolds) and anticlines (upfolds) in Ordovician shales and grits some 460 million years of age which occur along the foreshore; while at West Angle Bay you can see either side of a syncline in 350-million-year-old Carboniferous limestone on either side of the bay – the centre of the fold is in the middle of the bay.

ON THE BEACH

Beaches, dunes and mudflats are just as much a part of the geological landscape as cliffs and bays, but unlike 'solid' geological features, they are in a state of constant flux.

Beaches tend to be found where wave action is less severe, within bays or at the mouth of river valleys, or where the local geology is composed of soft, easily eroded rocks. Material is deposited from the sea, varying from sand through to shingle, pebbles and boulders. This material will be 'graded', so that the coarser material is found at the back of the beach and the finer material along the shoreline. This occurs as a direct result of wave action, with the heavier material being deposited further up the beach after storms, while the finer, lighter material is dragged back by the backwash, or falls out of suspension in calmer conditions.

You can see this at any beach in the area, although particularly good examples with impressive pebble banks at the top of the beach include Amroth, Freshwater West, Newgale and Abermawr.

Pembrokeshire's popular long, sandy beaches are often found along stretches of the coastline which are relatively sheltered from wave action compared to the surrounding coast, in areas where the waves are less energetic and smaller particles of material are deposited. This is not always the case though – beaches such as those of St Bride's Bay (Newgale, Nolton Haven, Druidston, Broad Haven and Little Haven) occur where the rocks are weak and easily eroded, allowing wave action to cut back into the strata and eventually form a series of sandy bays hemmed in by headlands of greater or lesser size.

CLIFF FEATURES

Some of the most impressive folding in the area occurs in the spectacular twisted and contorted cliffs of Cemaes Head, and you can see good examples of folding on a smaller scale in the coal measures at Settlands near Broad Haven. Here you can also see faulting, where the rocks either side of an obvious line have slipped and been displaced. This displacement may vary from centimetres to several kilometres, and examples can also be seen in the low cliffs at the south end of Whitesands Bay.

DROWNED FORESTS

You may see 'drowned forests' around the low tide line at some beaches. These occur at Amroth, Saundersfoot, Lydstep, Manorbier, Freshwater East, Freshwater West, Newgale, Whitesands, Abermawr and Newport, and are all that remain of a forest which was submerged when sea levels rose to their present level between 10,000 and 3,000 years ago. Immersion in salt water and burial under sand has helped to preserve the timber.

As you move out towards the more high-energy environments close to headlands, the beaches you find will be more shingly and rocky, reflecting the fact that they are made up of coarser material derived from nearby rocky headlands. An example of this is Ceibwr Bay near exposed Cemaes Head.

Beaches can markedly change in appearance over time. The large expanses of sand on which you walk or sunbathe in summer may be reduced to little more than rocks and boulders in winter, as a result of erosion by destructive waves. The storms and waves of winter remove much of the sand from the beach and drag it out to sea, exposing underlying rocks and giving the beach a steeper profile. Come the summer and the sand will be re-deposited on the beach in calmer conditions, covering the rocks and boulders and creating a gentler beach profile.

Behind many beaches, such as Newport and Freshwater East, you'll find sand dunes. These are fragile environments created from onshore winds blowing sand inland, where it may build up around an obstacle or rise in the land surface. Certain plants, marram grass in particular, can grow in this environment and their roots help to stabilise the dunes while the grass itself allows the build up of more sand. However, trampling can easily destroy this vegetation cover and lead to the erosion of the dunes.

Mud flats and salt marshes are found along more sheltered stretches of coastline, estuaries in particular, such as at the mouth of the River Teifi and the River Nevern, and along the sheltered inland waters of the Milford Haven waterway. These are also fragile environments, and they occur as a result of the deposition of river-borne sediments. Vegetation which is tolerant to submergence and salt water may eventually develop on the mud banks, leading to the formation of salt marshes – an important habitat for many bird species.

INLAND

Not all of Pembrokeshire's coastal geological features lie on the coast. If you look across Pembrokeshire from the vantage point of the Preseli Hills you'll notice that apart from the occasional isolated hill, the landscape is generally quite flat or gently undulating.

RAISED BEACHES

Another geological feature to be found in coastal environments is the 'raised' beach. These occur where the sea eroded the land surface when sea levels were higher, cutting a distinctive 'notch' or platform above present-day sea levels. These platforms generally have sand and pebbles deposited on their surface and are backed by cliffs. Good examples occur at Broad Haven South, Ogof Golchfa near Porthclais and Poppit Sands.

The St David's Peninsula and Ramsey Island, as well as the area south towards the Daugleddau Estuary, is a 'platform' at a relatively uniform height of 150-250ft (47-76m) apart from the obvious crags such as Carn Llidi, Carn Ysgubor, Penbiri and Carn Treglemais near St David's. A similar platform between 100-150ft (30-46m) occurs south of Milford Haven, and it is particularly obvious between Stackpole Head and Linney Head, while between Freshwater East and Lydstep Haven is a platform at a height of 197ft (60m) which extends out to Caldey Island.

These platforms are, in fact, erosion surfaces – huge wave-cut platforms - that developed when sea levels were much higher, and there are other, higher platforms in the area: one at 400ft (122m) around Hayscastle and another at 650ft (198m) on the southern fringe of the Preseli Hills.

The sea eroded indiscriminately across the landscape to form these platforms, irrespective of the resistance or complexity of the bedrock, thus unlike many other parts of Britain much of Pembrokeshire's landscape does not really reflect the underlying rock type and structure. In some ways the sea has had almost as much of an impact on the inland landscape as it has on the present-day coastline.

Higher ground which stands up above these platforms would have existed as islands during these periods of higher sea level, much as Ramsey, Skomer and Skokholm do today. These islands were generally made up of harder rocks which were resistant to sea erosion. Carn Llidi, Carn Ffald, Penbiri, Garn Fawr and Garn Gilfach, between St David's Head and Strumble Head, are all composed of resistant igneous rocks dating back over 440 million years to the Ordovician period.

Dating the surfaces of these wave-cut platforms is very difficult, as any associated beach material which may have given clues to the time when the erosion processes were taking place was removed by later erosion.

The Milford Haven waterway, on the other hand, was formed when the sea level was some 130ft (40m) lower than it is today, during the Ice Age when the sea

Above: Llaethdy: the lonely cottage below the craggy south-west slopes of Carn Llidi (595ft/181m) is now a youth hostel
Opposite: Wave-cut platform or 'raised beach' on the limestone cliffs near Lydstep Point
Below: The view across Dowrog Common towards the ancient 'islands' of Carn Perfedd (466ft/142m) and Carn Penberry (574ft/175m) demonstrates the sea-carved erosion platform around St David's

*Above: On the rhyolite pinnacle of
Maiden Castle above the Treffgarne
Gorge*

*Pages 30-1: Mynydd Preseli: amid
the strange outcrops of Carn Menyn
whence came the Stonehenge bluestones*

water was locked up in huge glaciers. Rivers excavated the Milford Haven waterway, the Daugleddau and other valleys, which were then submerged when sea
levels rose. There are smaller examples at Solva, Porth Clais and Aber Rhigian.

The sea has, however, had little to do with the development of the landscape of
the Preseli Hills and Gwaun Valley. The hills are composed of Ordovician shales
and mudstones transformed into slates, interspersed with volcanic intrusions of
rhyolite, volcanic ash and dolerite. The rocks here provided the early inhabitants
with axes, hammers and hoes, and most famously, the spotted dolerite from the
Carn Meini area was used to provide the inner ring of bluestones at Stonehenge.

The crags which rise above the gently rounded summits of the Preselis have
been subjected to millennia of weathering by frost and rain, particularly just
before, during, and immediately after, glacial periods. After the last glaciation, for
example, the ground would have been frozen for much of the year, and the
repeated freezing and thawing of water in cracks in the rocks led to frost-
shattering and the breaking up of the exposed strata.

The Gwaun Valley was formed as a result of glaciation, as a meltwater channel
running beneath melting ice masses. The River Gwaun which flows along the valley today is much too small for the size of its valley, which was carved out by far
larger volumes of meltwater towards the end of the last glaciation some 10,000
years ago, and also by earlier glaciations. Smaller meltwater channels include the
channel separating Dinas Island from the mainland, and that linking Porthgain
with Abereiddi.

Other glacial features in the area are less marked, and include boulder clay,
which was deposited in north Pembrokeshire and along the western coastline by

the Irish Sea ice sheet. This ice sheet affected the area between Cardigan and Fishguard and also crossed the St David's Peninsula to extend as far south as St Bride's Bay about 18,000 years ago. It deposited material scoured off the floor of the Irish Sea as well as boulders transported from as far away as Scotland. This material is widely spread over the landscape and partially fills some valleys, including those at Abermawr and Druidston Haven.

INDUSTRY

Coal was mined in Pembrokeshire from around 700 years ago to the early twentieth century. Although this was high-quality anthracite, geological problems, lack of investment and difficulties in transportation led to the demise of the industry by 1948. Coal was extracted in the Nolton Haven area, around Little Haven and Broad Haven, between Saundersfoot and Amroth, and in places along the Daugleddau Estuary, particularly Hook. At most of these locations the adits and bell pits can still be seen. Some of these – around Broad Haven and Little Haven, for example - may date back to the Middle Ages.

As is so often the case with coal mining, danger was never far away and in 1845 the first national mining disaster took place at Garden Pit, Landshipping, when the River Cleddau burst into the workings and more than forty men and boys, some as young as nine, were drowned.

Iron ore was also mined on a small scale from the cliff face between Saundersfoot and Amroth, and the presence of local coal and the 'tram road' to Saundersfoot Harbour saw the building of an iron works at Stepaside in 1849. This only survived until 1877, although a foundry at Wiseman's Bridge was in operation until 1926.

Slate quarrying in north Pembrokeshire reached its peak in the nineteenth century, although there is evidence that it was taking place at least as far back as the early seventeenth century. The largest quarry in the area was Rosebush in the Preseli Hills, which employed over eighty men in the 1870s, and although no longer working the quarry is still a major feature of the local landscape. The remains of over 120 quarries can be found across the north Pembrokeshire landscape, including a number of 'sea quarries', none more spectacular than Abereiddi's 'Blue Lagoon', which was flooded by the sea at the end of its working days.

In the sixteenth century, copper was extracted on the mainland coast opposite Ramsey Island from one of the most dramatically situated mines in Britain. However, this was a short-lived enterprise. Nearby, the attractive purple Caerbwdi sandstone, of which St David's Cathedral and Bishop's Palace are partly built, was extracted from the bay of the same name.

At Porthgain the landscape was ravaged by the quarrying of slate, shale and andesite (for road stone) in the nineteenth and early twentieth century, and at one time over 100 ships were registered here to transport these materials and locally-made bricks. These industries died out due to high running costs, and time has mellowed the effects of all this industry. Today the harbour's industrial heritage provides plenty of character and sits surprisingly well in the surrounding coastline.

On the whole, Pembrokeshire has seen little large-scale use made of its geological reserves, leaving a landscape largely unmarked by quarrying and mining.

CHIMNEYS AND PILLOWS

The Three Chimneys, Marloes, are horizontal beds of rock of Silurian Age (410-440 million years BP) which have been tilted vertically by powerful earth movements.

Pillow lava occurs when lava from a volcanic eruption is extruded underwater or when it flows from the land into the sea. The rapid cooling of the lava results in globular masses of lava which pile up one on top of the other before solidifying, to resemble pillows. Good examples occur at Porth Maenmelyn near Garn Fawr and at Strumble Head.

Below: The sea has entered the abandoned quarry working at Aber Eiddy to form the Blue Lagoon, where a coasteering party is seen having fun

2 Climate, vegetation and wildlife

The air of this county is ... found to be very healthy to the county's inhabitants.

George Owen, *The Description of Pembrokeshire*, 1603

FLOWERS OF THE COAST

There is no month during which some form of flower won't be in bloom, whether it be the ubiquitous bright yellow gorse of the cliff tops and hills: the paler yellow primroses in hedge banks and gardens, or the blanket of summer colour along the Coast Path from wildflowers such as sea campion, spring squill, kidney vetch, thrift, sea pink, oxeye daisy and many, many others.

Pembrokeshire has one of the mildest climates in the British Isles due to its position, surrounded by sea on three sides, and the fact that the sea itself is far warmer than might be expected at this latitude, as a result of the moderating effects of the Gulf Stream. It also occupies a unique geographical position where species typical of northern cold waters and Mediterranean waters overlap.

Some of the habitats, in particular those of the islands, sea cliffs and coastal waters, are of worldwide importance. Grassholm, Skomer and Skokholm have international designations as Special Protection Areas on account of their important seabird colonies, while the coast at Castlemartin has a similar designation because of its chough population.

Opposite top: Above Bull Hole on the north-west coast of Skomer
Opposite below: Wildflowers, Penbwchdy Head
Right: Strumble peninsula west coast
Below: Green lane near St Nicholas (Tremarchog) in spring

There are also four National Nature Reserves within the park (Ty Canol, Pengelli Forest, Skomer Island and Stackpole), and a 10 square mile (27sq km) area of sea and sea bed around Skomer Island which makes up one of only three Marine Nature Reserves in the UK.

Pembrokeshire's coastal location also means that not only does it have some of the most impressive and varied seabird colonies in Britain, it is also a stopping-off place for many different migratory birds. Larger sea life is also many and varied and includes grey seals, porpoises, dolphins, basking sharks and occasional exotic species such as sunfish.

CLIMATE

Extremes of weather, other than gales and storms, are rare – in fact a cold day in summer may be almost the same temperature as a 'warm' day in winter. Snowfall seldom occurs outside the Preseli Hills, and the same is true of frost, which is obviously a great advantage for local farmers. Even in the Preselis, snow seldom remains on the ground for more than a few days at a time.

Spring and autumn can give you all four seasons in the space of a few days. For instance, it's not unknown in April for snow to fall on the hills one day while the next day people may be sunbathing on the beach. Despite this unpredictability, spring and autumn are excellent seasons for visiting the area; if you catch the weather right there's nothing to compare with exploring the coast and hills on a warm day in May or October, with hardly anyone else around.

Summers are pleasantly warm, with average temperatures along the coast around 18 degrees C, and 2 or 3 degrees warmer inland. A heat wave will rarely last longer than a few days in all but the best of summers, and when the weather does turn, it can often be to a gentle refreshing rain drifting in off the Atlantic

*Above: The lifeboat station at Porth
Justinian on Ramsey Sound*

which isn't at all cold or particularly unpleasant. Even when it's hot, you often get a gentle onshore breeze to take the edge off things.

Dale is the sunniest place in Wales, and the St David's and Castlemartin peninsulas have similar sunshine totals. The driest months tend to be April, May and June, and the Dale peninsula has some of the lowest rainfall figures in South Wales, with an average annual total of 31in (787mm). This increases noticeably as you go inland where the moisture-laden winds blowing in off the sea are forced to rise over higher land, thus unloading their water. Haverfordwest, for instance, has 45in (1,143mm) of rain per year, and the Preseli Hills more than 60in (1,524mm).

The one thing that any visitor is likely to notice about the weather, though, is the wind. On average Pembrokeshire experiences thirty-two gales per year (winds in excess of 40 mph/60 km/hr), and storm-force winds (over 64 mph/103 km/hr) are not unusual on the coast.

These can result in some of the most spectacular sights, when headlands of 65ft (20m) or more in height will be totally submerged beneath huge swells. It's under these conditions that you can readily understand how the Pembrokeshire coastline has come to be littered with shipwrecks over the centuries, and how the services provided by RNLI lifeboats and their crew, the coastguard and the various lighthouses (now all automatic) along the coast continue to be an important feature of life for many communities within the Park and for individuals out on the open seas.

The wild storms which may lead to the call-out of a lifeboat may also result in structural damage to buildings, and the few trees and bushes on Pembrokeshire's exposed headlands and hills are often bent and twisted into bizarre shapes by these fierce, salt-laden winds.

Like the local air temperatures, the temperature of the sea doesn't fluctuate too wildly with the seasons, thanks to the Gulf Stream. In summer inshore waters may reach 16 degrees C, maybe a little warmer, whilst in winter the temperature rarely drops below 7-8 degrees C. This allows rare northern coral species to grow off Skomer Island, and the less rare northern surfers, divers and windsurfers to enjoy their sport year-round. In good summers, species from further south may drift north with the warm currents – sunfish, mako sharks and seahorses are just three examples which have been seen in Pembrokeshire's waters.

If you're planning on getting out into those same waters, one thing to bear in mind is that the sea warms and cools more slowly than the land, so if you're enjoying a heat wave in May don't expect the sea to be warm too. You'll have to wait until late August/early September for it to reach its most pleasant temperature.

VEGETATION

Pembrokeshire's mild climate allows vegetation to thrive year-round. There are sections of the Coast Path in the south of the county, for instance, where the annual growth on either side of the path would be several metres in height were it not regularly cut back to allow access for walkers. In this part of the Park you'll also find palm trees are quite common – not a native species, of course, but well able to survive here thanks to the mild climate.

A combination of the close proximity of the sea and the predominantly lowland landscape has had a major influence on species and habitats, many of which are restricted to Pembrokeshire's mild western oceanic environment. Another unique feature of the landscape is that unlike the other National Parks of England and Wales, up to 70 per cent of the land is intensively farmed, which obviously is an important factor affecting vegetation and wildlife.

One of the best-known features of the coastline is the cheerful display of wildflowers in early summer. A patchwork of colours spreads out over the clifftops and

JEWELS OF SUMMER

With the flowers come butterflies such as dark green fritillaries, skippers and common blues. Although the colourful display of wildflowers fades away in midsummer, the vibrant yellow gorse and rich purple heather of the coastal slopes and hills bring colour back to the coastal headlands in late summer.

Left: Wildflowers, Penbwchdy Head
Right: A roadside bank in the Solva valley in mid-May

Above: The famed surfing beach at Freshwater West is seen over the dunes of Broomhill Burrows. Still-forbidden Linney Head, the western extremity of the limestone Castlemartin coast, is seen beyond

TIME AND TIDES

Pembrokeshire has some of the greatest tidal ranges in the world. The difference between high and low water on the biggest, or spring, tides may be as much as 26ft (8m). (Spring tides, incidentally, occur twice a month at full and new moons, and not just in the spring.) On the smallest, or neap tides (also twice a month at half moon) this difference can be less than 16ft (5m).

along either side of the Coast Path in late May and early June. White sea campion, yellow and red kidney vetch, violet-blue spring squill, pink thrift, bright white and yellow oxeye daisy, orange-red bird's-foot trefoil, cobalt bluebells and red campion are just a few of the flowers that blanket stretches of the coastline and make a coastal walk in early summer a really exhilarating experience. Rare flowering plants may also be found on mainland cliffs, including some species of rock lavender, Newport centaury, wild chives and spiked speedwell.

The Atlantic breezes keep the air invigoratingly clear and healthy all year round, as can be seen from the rich array of lichens on cliffs, walls and buildings and in woodlands – indicators of good air quality.

In many areas of the National Park farmers traditionally grazed their stock right up to the edge of the sea cliffs and coastal slopes, such as above St Bride's Bay and on the Dale Peninsula. The decline of this method of farming has led to the loss of internationally important habitats such as maritime heath and sea-cliff grassland, and an associated decline in key species like the chough. In recent years, the National Park Authority has run grant-aid schemes to encourage farmers to return to traditional techniques and help restore the biodiversity of the coastal slopes.

Beneath the cliffs, the intertidal zone is one of the harshest environments on Earth. Depending on the tides, all or part of this zone may be alternately submerged by sea water and exposed to air, rain and sunshine twice a day, and the various fish, shellfish, seaweeds and crustaceans which live here have to be able to withstand these extreme conditions, not to mention the action of waves and currents.

Sand dunes such as those behind the beaches at Newport, Whitesands, Freshwater West and Tenby are also a harsh environment, but a few specialised plants survive here. The foredunes behind the tide rack support sea rocket, prickly saltwort and sea beet, which use rotting seaweed as a source of humus. Sea couch-grass, and behind this marram grass, can survive in the deeper sand of the main dunes thanks to long roots which can tap water supplies. At the same time the roots provide an anchor for sand accumulation. Further back in the dune system plants such as sand sedge, spurges, bee orchid, pyramidal orchid and lichens can be found. This is a fragile environment that is easily destroyed by trampling, and at most dune systems access is restricted to prevent damage.

One of the most fascinating creatures to live close to or within the grassed areas of dune systems is the adder. These beautifully marked snakes are timid by nature and, while poisonous, will not strike unless threatened. Indeed, on the very day that I'm writing this a large adder – over a foot in length – fell down a grassy bank and landed at my feet while I was walking barefoot along the path through the dunes above Whitesands. I don't know who got the greater surprise, but the adder was certainly the quickest to make a rapid retreat!

While not extensive, Pembrokeshire's woodland areas can be delightful places to enjoy an easy walk, particularly in autumn or when gales are blowing on the coast and you're seeking some shelter. In recent years they have been much more sensitively managed by organisations such as the National Park Authority, Coed Cymru and the Forestry Authority, to make them more attractive both for people and wildlife. Areas of semi-natural woodland such as the Gwaun Valley, the Nevern Valley and the Daugleddau provide a rich habitat for species such as badger, fox, rabbit and weasel, and along the river valleys of the Gwaun and Nevern, otters are also known to breed.

Below: Hikers in the bluebell woods of Pen-yr-allt: this is the approach path to Aber Mawr bay, near St Nicholas

Above: Mountain ponies graze the southern slopes of Mynydd Dinas above Cwm Gwaun

The trail around the ancient woodland of Ty Canol, near Nevern, gives you some idea of how this part of the Pembrokeshire landscape would have looked when the people who originally erected the Iron Age settlement at Castell Henllys lived here.

Above Ty Canol lie the Preseli Hills, a very different environment to that of lowland Pembrokeshire. A large swathe of the lower slopes of the hills is made up of coniferous forest, not a particularly species-rich habitat, while the open, exposed moorland above is home to hardy Welsh mountain ponies. Several mountain bike journeys across the Preseli Hills then down to the coast have given me a good feel for the difference in climate which may occur between an elevation of almost 2,000ft (600m) and sea level. Fleece and waterproofs are required for the hill tops, T-shirt and shorts when you get down to the coast.

WILDLIFE

Pembrokeshire is perhaps best known for its bird life, in particular seabirds, with internationally important colonies of gannets, Manx shearwaters, storm petrel, chough and peregrine falcon.

The strong tidal currents and continual movement of waters around the coast stimulate the growth of marine plankton, a rich source of food which attracts many of the seabirds and is one of the main reasons for the great variety and number in the area.

Skomer, Skokholm and Middleholm Island between them have some 150,000 pairs of Manx shearwaters - the world's largest breeding population. Shearwaters nest in underground burrows and are only active at night, spending the day either in the burrow incubating their single egg or out at sea feeding, but they can be

seen on summer evenings gathering in large 'rafts' out at sea.

Puffins are also to be found on these same islands, and elsewhere in lesser numbers, and they too live in underground burrows. You'll very rarely find either puffins or shearwaters on the mainland, because living in burrows makes them easy prey for mammals such as rats, foxes and stoats. Rats in particular are the reason for their absence from Cardigan Island, Ramsey, Caldey and St Margaret's Island.

Grassholm Island, 7 miles (11km) offshore, has the world's fourth largest gannetry, with some 33,000 breeding pairs. The colony can be seen from shore as a white 'snow' patch on the island, and these magnificent, brilliant white birds which catch their fish by diving, are occasionally seen close to shore. A trip out to Grassholm by boat offers an unforgettable wildlife sight – and smell!

Other birds to be found on island and coastal cliffs include cormorants and shags, which tend live on cliff slopes and larger ledges. They're too big to land or sit comfortably on narrow ledges and are poor at taking off from level ground. Cormorants and shags have a similar appearance, but you can tell the difference from the fact that cormorants often stand on rocks holding their wings out, as if to dry them.

Smaller cliff ledges may be occupied by razorbills (the bird on the National Park logo), where they build their cup-shaped nests of mud and seaweed, and guillemots. Razorbills tend to nest in individual pairs while guillemots crowd together and may form large and impressive colonies huddled on long rock shelves on sea stacks, islands and cliffs. Their eggs are very conical in shape,

Above: A birdwatcher studies puffins above the Wick, an important nesting site on the southern coast of Skomer

Below: Puffins on Skomer

which reduces the risk of them rolling off the ledge. Kittiwakes (named after the sound of their call) and fulmars also live on coastal cliffs on both the mainland and the islands, and feed close to their nesting sites.

Those birds which live on mainland cliffs within access of predators must be able to defend their nests. Gulls (herring gulls, lesser and great black-backed gulls and kittiwake) are usually quite capable of seeing off any threats, and greater black-backed gulls will also take the eggs and chicks of other seabirds. Fulmars have the delightful defence mechanism of regurgitating and ejecting the foul-smelling contents of their stomach over any animal or human getting too close to their nest.

Food resources obviously play a major role in determining the habitat for any bird, and sea fish and shellfish are the major sources of food for all the birds described here, other than the chough and other members of the crow family. Exceptions may include lesser and greater black-backed gulls and herring gulls, which often scavenge for food among litter bins and rubbish tips, and cormorants which may hunt for fish in estuaries and rivers as well as at sea.

Some species, such as Manx shearwater and storm petrels (which, like shearwaters, also live on the offshore islands), will go many miles out to sea in search of fish – shearwaters are known to fly as far south as the Bay of Biscay. For others, like oystercatchers and curlews, the opposite is true – they never travel far from the coastline, using their long beaks to probe the sand and mud along the seashore, to turn over pebbles, or to search ploughed fields close to the coast.

The Pembrokeshire coast is also the home to the second fastest bird on Earth, the peregrine falcon, which can dive for its prey - usually small birds - at speeds in

Above: Grey seal cub
Opposite: Manx shearwater
(All photographs pp42–3 by Melvin Grey)

Below: Peregrine falcon at the nest

excess of 120mph (190km/hr). In the Middle Ages, Ramsey peregrines were greatly valued by the nobility as hunting birds. Kestrels and buzzards may also be seen hovering in the sky both on the coast and inland.

Smaller birds to be found along the coast include the rock pipit and meadow pipit, while yellowhammers, stonechats and skylark are also quite common near to the coast and further inland.

Pembrokeshire's estuaries, with their mudbanks and shallow waters, are an ideal habitat for a number of species of wader and wildfowl. The Daugleddau Estuary in particular is an important habitat for resident and migratory species, including shelduck, grebe, dunlin, turnstone, ringed plover and redshank as well as oyster-catchers, cormorants and grey herons.

One of the most endearing creatures within the National Park is the grey seal. With the second largest colony in southern Britain, Ramsey Island is the best place to see adults, yearlings and, especially in autumn, white-furred seal pups. However, they also live elsewhere around the coast, including the readily accessible Deer Park near Marloes, and it's not unusual to spot a grey seal or two bobbing about in the water and watching you as you walk along the cliff tops.

Schools of porpoise, and less commonly dolphin, are often seen off Ramsey, Skokholm and Skomer, and if you can't get out to the islands you may also be lucky and spot them from headlands such as Strumble and St David's Head.

Bigger species, in particular the huge basking shark, which is the world's second largest fish and feeds exclusively on plankton, are also occasionally seen, although ideally you need to be in a boat to spot this and rarer creatures such as pilot whales, killer whales, sun fish and various species of sharks.

CHOUGHS AND CROWS

Caves, holes and cracks in cliffs may be occupied by jackdaws and choughs both on the mainland and offshore. Choughs (above) are rare in most other parts of Britain, and are an easily recognised member of the crow family, given away by their bright red beak and legs. Crows and ravens, members of the same family as the chough, can be seen in large flocks both inland and on the coast.

THE FOUR SEASONS

No time of year is the wrong time to visit Pembrokeshire – there's always something to see. Here are some brief natural highlights of what's on show along the coastline throughout the year.

January – Flowers such as campion and gorse will be still out. Fulmars will be wheeling around the cliffs and guillemots and razorbills can be seen in inshore waters.

February – Spectacular display flights of chough, ravens and crows along the coast as a prelude to the breeding season. First violets appear in more sheltered bays, and skylarks sing on warmer days.

March – The first migrants arrive onshore, wheatears and sandmartins pass overhead, later followed by swallows. In mild years, thrift will be flowering by the end of the month.

April – Start of nesting season for many coastal birds. Thrift, spring squill, kidney vetch and bird's-foot trefoil are all in flower.

May & June – The breeding season is in full swing for birds, and Coast Path flowers are at their brightest and most impressive. There are plenty of butterflies towards the end of June.

July – Seals start to be seen more frequently close to shore. Young choughs flock and forage in groups of up to twenty or thirty. Watch out for adders sunning themselves on the Coast Path.

August – The first seal pups are born, and seals become quite common around the mainland coast. The headlands of Strumble, St Davids and Deer Park are alive with the lemon-yellow gorse and rich purple heather.

September – Seal pupping is in full swing, and adult females may sometimes be heard calling as you walk by. Autumn bird migration is well under way with sometimes thousands of seabirds passing headlands such as Strumble as they head south for the winter. The first of the autumn/winter gales are likely to lash the coast around now. Young fulmars leave their nests to moult out at sea.

October – Seal pupping coming to an end. On estuaries and embayments such as Angle Bay and the Gann, wader and wildfowl numbers increase markedly as they move in for the winter.

November & December – Fulmars return to cliffs after their moult. Occasionally flowers such as red campion are seen in flower, and small groups of choughs may be seen feeding on cliff tops.

Right: Evening view from Maidenhall Point over St Bride's Bay towards the skerries of Black Scar and Green Scar

3 Man's influence

Everywhere you feel the presence of the megalithic tomb builders, of the Iron Age warriors who piled their stones for the great hill forts and of the kindly and absent-minded old Celtic saints.

Wynford Vaughan Thomas on the Preseli Hills, in *Countryside Companion*, 1979

Opposite above & below: The crom-lechs (Neolithic burial chambers) of Carreg Samson (top), and King's Quoit, on Priest's Nose
Below: A prehistoric hut circle near the southernmost point of Skomer

Pembrokeshire's rich history is imprinted firmly on its landscape and this is apparent as soon as you start to explore the Park. Sites such as Pentre Ifan in the Preseli Hills, Pembroke and Carew Castles and St David's Cathedral are the obvious lodestones to the past, but much of the area's history is also present in smaller and lesser-known sites which are just as fascinating.

The earliest signs of mankind in Pembrokeshire date back some 20,000 years, in the form of flint tools and discarded animal bones of the Old Stone Age (Palaeolithic) period, found on Caldey Island, at Cat's Hole Cave near Monkton and Hoyle's Mouth Cave near Tenby. Middle Stone Age (Mesolithic) flint chippings have also been found at Nab Head near St Brides (including rare shale beads), at the spectacular cave known as The Wogan in Pembroke Castle, on the banks of the Afon Nyfer at Newport, and near Solva.

However, it wasn't until the New Stone Age (Neolithic) some 5,000 years ago that Pembrokeshire's landscape began to see the development of monuments which survive to this day. Although the only signs of actual settlements left by New Stone Age people are limited to caves on Caldey and at Clegyr Boia near St David's, their cromlechs, or burial chambers, are evocative and resonant signatures of their presence in the area. These include the impressive Pentre Ifan on the northern slopes of the Preseli Hills, and Carreg Samson near Abercastle, while the King's Quoit at Manorbier is literally beside the Coast Path, so you can't miss it.

Coastal and elevated locations such as St David's Head, Newport Bay and the Preseli Hills were popular sites for these burial chambers. They typically consist of two or more huge stone slabs supporting a massive capstone. This structure would have been covered with rocks and soil to create a huge tumulus, although in some instances the covering would only reach as far as the capstone. The most enduring mystery left by these people originated (in part at least) in the Preseli Hills, but now rests on Salisbury Plain in England in the form of eighty 'bluestones', each weighing up to 4 tons, which form the inner circle and 'horseshoe' of Stonehenge. The 'bluestones' consist of spotted dolerite, rhyolite and volcanic ash from the eastern Preseli Hills. No one has yet proved decisively how they got there.

Pages 48-9: The magnificent Neolithic cromlech of Pentre Ifan stands on the northern slopes of the Mynydd Preseli near Brynberian

From this time on, burial mounds became an increasingly common landscape feature. Bronze Age people left a number of round cairns on elevated land such as

Above: There is a wide view from Carningli Common over Newport Bay to the headland of Pen-y-Bal Opposite: Inscribed in ogham text, this enigmatic fifth-century stone pillar stands beside St Brynac church, Nevern

CASTELL HENLLYS

The National Park Authority owns an award-winning reconstructed Iron Age settlement at Castell Henllys near Newport. At the only site of its kind in Britain, traditional roundhouses have been built on what was originally the site of an Iron Age hill fort, following excavations by archaeologists.

the Ridgeway between Tenby and Pembroke and Foel Drygarn in the Preseli Hills. Using their metal tools they also continued the clearance of the area's woodlands and forests which had been begun by their Neolithic forebears to allow farming of cereals and grazing of domesticated animals such as sheep, goats and pigs.

However it wasn't until the Iron Age, some 2,500 years ago, that there were major architectural and cultural impacts on the area. Iron Age people left the remnants of their settlements and fortifications, and their language may be related to present-day Welsh. They used hill tops and coastal and inland promontories as the locations for their forts and settlements because these were good defensive sites, and remains can be seen at various locations in the National Park, such as Carn Ingli above Newport, The Gribin on Solva Head, Deer Park, Marloes, and on St David's Head where the people living in the latter settlement also created a system of low-walled fields below Carn Llidi, some of which are still in use today.

It was probably around the eighth to sixth century BC that Celtic culture became firmly established in the British Isles and Pembrokeshire. Even with the coming of the Romans in the first century AD, the Celts in west Wales remained largely unaffected by this outside influence – there is little evidence that the Roman invasion of Britain had any major cultural impact on Pembrokeshire. However, they did have an economic impact on the area – recent excavations have

revealed a Roman road near Whitland that heads directly towards the west, indicating that the Romans may have used this as a trade route to the coast.

Initially the Celts were pagan, practising Druidic rites and celebrations such as the autumn festival of Samhain, which has been handed down to us as Hallowe'en. Druidism incorporated various bloody practices; the Roman historian Cornelius Tacitus tells of the altars of Welsh Druids being drenched in human blood after some of their ceremonies. Some of the Celts' myths, stories and legends were later recorded in *The Mabinogion*, a collection of anonymous stories that were part of an older oral tradition incorporating Celtic mythology and folklore and the Arthurian legends.

The area is also thought to have seen an Irish dynasty installed around the fifth century after a series of devastating raids on the west coast of Wales. Little evidence of these people is seen today other than the occasional stone inscribed in ogham script, a form of writing which originated in Ireland. Good examples can be seen at religious sites in Nevern and on Caldey.

With the coming of Christianity – which was quite well-established by the 'Age of Saints' in the fifth to sixth centuries – both Celtic and Christian cultures became intermingled. Society was extremely hierarchical; rulers of great power at the top of the tree were followed by noblemen and freemen who owed their ruler services

Pages 52-3: An Iron Age hill fort crowns the Gribin Ridge at Solva, traversed on the Pembrokeshire Coast Path

and who also held rights in the arable and grazing land, and finally the majority, the bondsmen who worked the land. Many settlements would be clustered around the seat – or *llys* – of the lord where bondsmen farmed and laboured on his behalf.

Unfortunately there are few traces of this period to be seen today – early Christian churchyards and inscribed stones, and various place names, are the only readily accessible reminders. During the Age of Saints, monks from Ireland and the continent travelled throughout Wales to reinforce Christianity, and there are several Christian stones scattered around Pembrokeshire. The most impressive are actually from a later period, occurring in the form of late tenth and early eleventh century crosses at Nevern, Penally and Carew, which display classic interlaced designs and Latin inscriptions.

These early missionaries, many of whom became saints, built small coastal chapels as thanksgiving for safe delivery from the perils of ocean travel, their main form of transport being frail skin boats. These monastic cells became churches dedicated to Celtic saints such as David, Brynach, Padarn and Teilo.

Pembrokeshire, and the St David's area in particular, seems to have held a great attraction for the early saints – St David, his mother St Non, St Patrick and St Justinian all have chapels named after them on the coastline around the St David's Peninsula, and all are situated at or close to landing places used by early pilgrims. St David founded a monastery at Ty Gwyn, above Whitesands Bay, in the sixth century, before transferring it to Glyn Rhoson where the present-day cathedral is located in the shelter of the Alun Valley, where it could avoid detection from marauding Norse invaders (they sacked the cathedral several times and in 999 murdered its bishop).

St David is said to have died on 1 March (now St David's Day) 588, and his bones, along with those of St Justinian, his confessor, reputedly lie in the cathedral.

Whatever the truth of the St David's myths and legends, the man himself was canonised by Pope Callixtus II (1119-24), after which two pilgrimages to St David's Cathedral were accepted as the equivalent of one to Rome.

Between the ninth and eleventh centuries the Vikings launched savage raids on the area from their bases in Ireland and the Isle of Man. The major islands were named by the Norsemen (Caldey, Skomer, Skokholm, Middleholm, Grassholm

and Ramsey) as well as a number of settlements such as Fishguard (Fisgard), Solva, Musselwick, Gelliswick, Dale and Tenby (Daneby). One of the most regular 'visitors' was Hubba, who overwintered with twenty-three warships in Milford Haven in 877-8. The village of Hubberston is said to have taken its name from him.

The medieval period saw the church and military become increasingly important in Pembrokeshire. After their success at the Battle of Hastings in 1066, the Normans quickly spread across southern Britain and by the end of the eleventh century they were occupying south Pembrokeshire. Prior to this the Welsh prince Rhys ap Tewdwr ruled the principality of Deheubarth (south-west Wales), eventually paying tribute to William the Conqueror, who made a pilgrimage to St David's in 1081, at the same time establishing his overlordship of the area.

With the death of Rhys in 1093, the Normans increased their control of much of Wales, and built the first Welsh castles in what was known as *pura Wallia* (pure or non-Norman Wales). Initially these were motte-and-bailey castles of earth and timber, and little remains of these in Pembrokeshire other than the earthworks, or mottes. The bailey was the fortified area on top of the motte, which was surrounded by a ditch and palisade. Remains of such castles can be seen at New Moat, Maenclochog, Wiston and Nevern.

The better-sited of these castles were eventually rebuilt in stone, so that the earthworks and mounds which remain today generally indicate sites that were abandoned. Of the new stone castles that developed from the eleventh century on, Pembroke is the most impressive and commanding. Its strategic position on a high ridge between two tidal inlets was chosen early in the first Norman incursions into south-west Wales, Roger de Montgomery founding the castle in 1093. In the twelfth century Pembroke Castle was an important embarkation point for Norman raids on Ireland, and between 1189-1219 William Marshal developed it from an earth-and-timber structure to a literally impregnable stone fortress - the castle never fell to Welsh attacks.

The Normans were also responsible for developing a chain of castles across south-west Wales that marked the 'Landsker', a word of Norse origin signifying a frontier. To the north of this were the native 'Welshry', to the south the Normans and Anglo-Saxons moved in (later becoming known as the 'Englishry'), taking the

MYTHS OF ST DAVID

Many myths surround St David and his contemporaries; an example of one that brings in most of the cultural and spiritual influences of the time is St David's fight to win over to Christianity the Celtic chieftain Boia (after which Clegyr Boia near St David's is named). David succeeded in converting the chieftain's people, but Boia himself is said to have been struck down by lightning – or slaughtered by the Irish pirate Liski (whose name is perpetuated in nearby Porthlysgi). Take your pick as to which one is true ...

Opposite top: Carew Cross (AD1035) commemorates Maredudd ap Edwin, a local king
Opposite below left: Eleventh-century High Cross in St Brynach churchyard at Nevern
Opposite below right: Evening view near Porthlysgi
Below: Pembroke Castle (AD1190) is surrounded on three sides by a tidal moat

THE LANDSKER LINE

The Landsker Line was marked in Pembrokeshire by the castles of Roch, Haverfordwest, Picton, Wiston, Llawhaden, Narberth and Amroth. To the north Welsh culture and the Welsh language were and still are a major feature of everyday life, while to the south – known for centuries as 'Little England Beyond Wales' – the English language and customs predominate. As recently as 1957, author and naturalist R.M. Lockley remarked in his book Pembrokeshire *that marriages between people from north and south Pembrokeshire were not that frequent, and that the register of electors showed a marked preponderance of Welsh names in the north – Jones, Williams, Davies, Evans and Thomas - and English names – Allen, Skyrme, Greenslade, Hathaway, Mirehouse, Warlow, Belton, Beynon and White – in the south. To a noticeable extent this is still the case today.*

better agricultural land for themselves and forcing the Welsh onto the generally poorer quality terrain of north Pembrokeshire. The south also saw the arrival early in the twelfth century of Flemings who had been driven to Britain after the flooding of their low-lying homeland.

Place names in the south are predominantly English, and churches tend to possess Norman-style tall square towers which served for centuries as lookouts, while in the north place names are more commonly Welsh and churches tend to be small, towerless buildings with bellcotes. Later, chapels became common as the Non-conformist movement developed more strongly in north Pembrokeshire in the nineteenth century.

The Normans developed a number of castles and settlements south of the Landsker Line – Manorbier and Carew are good examples. A notable feature of their siting was that they were often close to the sea, the major highway of the time. Manorbier Castle is famous as the birthplace of Giraldus Cambrensis, who wrote of his travels around Wales in 1188 in *The Itinerary through Wales*, in which he described his birthplace as 'the pleasantest spot in Wales' – and many would still agree with that description today.

Carew, which was originally an Iron Age fort then a Dark Age stronghold, was eventually made into an impressive fortified home by owners such as the de Carew family, Rhys ap Thomas and Sir John Perrot, the latter responsible for the 'north wing' with its superb mullioned windows. The whole of this impressive Elizabethan country house has been consolidated in recent years by the National Park Authority and CADW: Welsh Historic Monuments.

Tenby also developed around its castle, and today displays 900 years of architecture – Norman castle, medieval town walls including the Five Arches and Tudor Merchant's House, Regency features including the Laston House baths built by William Caxton in 1810-11, and Edwardian and Victorian houses and hotels.

St David's, on the other hand, developed around its cathedral and Bishop's Palace in the eleventh and twelfth centuries to become the ecclesiastical centre of

Above: The ancient Landsker Line followed the Brandy Brook, seen here at Newgale
Right: Carew Castle, north-west aspect
Opposite: Roch Castle, now a private residence, is seen from the east against a thundery dusk

Wales. The construction of the cathedral was begun around 1180 by Bishop Peter de Leia. The Bishop's Palace dates from around 1350 and was built by Bishop Henry de Gower. Its roof was stripped of lead in 1536 by Bishop Barlow who wanted the seat of the St David's bishopric removed to Carmarthen. After this it rapidly fell into disrepair. St David's Cathedral and the Bishop's Palace is one of the most evocative and historic sites in Wales and is still worth a pilgrimage today, whatever your religious leanings.

Bishop Gower was also responsible for expanding Lamphey Bishop's Palace into a magnificent residence during the fourteenth century. A survey of 1326 known as the *Black Book of St David's* describes the productive lands of the manor. The bishops of St David's also had a castle at Llawhaden. This was surrounded by particularly rich ecclesiastical estates, and Llawhaden Castle, developed mainly in the late thirteenth and early fourteenth century by Bishop Thomas Bek and Bishop David Martyn, was built to protect these. Several of the bishops of St David's of this time also held high national office - Bishop Bek, for example, was Keeper of the King's Wardrobe and Chancellor of Oxford University.

Despite its relative isolation, throughout the Middle Ages Pembrokeshire periodically became involved with affairs affecting the rest of Wales and England. The uprisings against English rule by the Welsh princes Llewellyn the Great and his

Above: The tower of St David's Cathedral rises over the trees in its green hollow below the little town
Left: The imposing gatehouse of Llawhaden Castle towers over the village street

PEMBROKESHIRE IN THE CIVIL WAR

Pembrokeshire was drawn into battle during the English Civil War. When King Charles and the Royalists took up arms against Cromwell in 1642, they used several Welsh castles as bases. During the second war of 1648 Pembroke Castle was held for Parliament until the end of the conflict when the leaders Poyer, Powell and Laugharne changed sides, only to be defeated by Cromwell. In fact Cromwell personally directed the bombardment of the castle, and after the war Parliament ordered the partial destruction of Pembroke Castle — and other castles throughout the kingdom — to prevent it being used militarily again. Tenby Castle also underwent a siege of ten weeks during the Civil War, and Carew Castle changed hands three times.

grandson Llewllyn the Last in the thirteenth century, and by Owain Glyndwr in the early fifteenth century, had little effect on Pembrokeshire (although Tenby was sacked by Llewllyn the Last in 1260), but Wales did supply an 'English' king in the form of Henry Tudor, earl of Richmond, who was born in Pembroke Castle in 1457.

In 1485, during the Wars of the Roses, Henry returned from refuge in France to land at Mill Bay on the Dale Peninsula from where he marched to Bosworth Field to defeat Richard III and the House of York and take the throne of England as Henry VII. His son, Henry VIII, fortified Milford Haven and established the boundaries of Pembrokeshire as they were to remain for over 400 years.

For most people, however, life in Pembrokeshire revolved around farming, fishing or seafaring. Coastal trading was particularly important from the Elizabethan period on, especially along the Bristol Channel, across the Irish Sea and along the coast of western Europe. Coal from the Pembrokeshire coalfields was exported and lime from south Pembrokeshire went to farms in the north of the county as well as elsewhere in Britain (there were few quays and harbours in the area without lime kilns, and many can still be seen today, such as at Porthclais and Solva). Woollen cloth, hides, slates, herrings, oysters, corn, malt and hides were also exported, while imports included salt, fruit, tobacco, timber, millstones and wine.

Rural industries included woollen mills, corn mills and wood turning, and the elegant Blackpool Mill (1813) on the Eastern Cleddau can still be visited, as can Carew French Mill, one of only three restored tidal mills in Britain.

Pembrokeshire also holds the distinction of being the site of the last invasion of Britain, when in 1797 a motley crew of French 'soldiers' (many were released convicts) came ashore at Carregwastad Point near Fishguard under the command of the Irish-American General Tate. According to tradition the invaders were tricked into surrender by the distant sight of massed ranks of soldiers ready to defend their homeland who were, in fact, local women in traditional stovepipe hats and scarlet mantles. Just how much truth there is in this is open to question.

Around this period the influence of Non-conformism was also making itself felt in Pembrokeshire, with religious dissent and disaffection persisting throughout

Above: The tiny church of St Gwyndaf at Llanwdna is associated with the French landings in 1797 on nearby Carregwastad Point

Opposite top: This lonely chimney on the undercliff above St Bride's Bay is all that remains of Trefrane Colliery near Nolton Haven
Opposite below: Old lime kilns stand beside the sheltered harbour at Solva

the seventeenth, eighteenth and nineteenth centuries. Examples include Lewis David and his fellow Quakers who fled to Pennsylvania in 1686, where they founded the towns of Milford and Narberth, while John Wesley was a regular visitor to the county.

With its location on the western edge of the British Isles, the strategic importance of the Milford Haven waterway was recognised by Admiral Lord Nelson in 1802, who described the port as one of the finest harbours in the world, and from 1814–1926 Pembroke Dock was the site of the Royal Dockyard. For a short-lived period at the turn of the nineteenth century, Neyland and Fishguard saw transatlantic liners calling in on their way to the United States, and Milford Haven was a major UK fishing port in the early twentieth century.

Pembrokeshire's location on the western approaches also meant that it always had seaward-facing defences, from the forts and castles of Celts and Normans to more high-tech structures of the nineteenth and twentieth centuries. These include the Martello towers erected in the Haven against possible attack by Napoleon III; the World War II flying-boat bases at Pembroke Dock; the airfields of the same period on the Dale Peninsula and at St David's (now being restored to nature by the National Park Authority), and the Castlemartin Artillery Range in south Pembrokeshire, which is still used for training by British and allied forces.

From the Industrial Revolution on Pembrokeshire became more accessible - Brunel was responsible for the development of the railway lines that brought the world to west Wales by land rather than sea for the first time. In the nineteenth century the first tourists found their way to Pembrokeshire, Tenby in particular, and with constantly improving access ever since an area that much of the world passed by for millennia has found its isolation becoming less and less marked.

However, the designation of the Pembrokeshire Coast National Park in 1952 meant that the inevitable development that came along with this increased access has not been able to go ahead regardless. All the same, as R.M. Lockley remarked in 1957, only five years after the National Park came into being: 'It is a considerable responsibility to call the attention of the world to an area of such unspoilt wildness and beauty, and then both encourage visitors to it and at the same time defend it from spoliation by those visitors.'

Only time will tell how well that responsibility has been shouldered, but for now, while nothing ever stays the same, it's true to say that you can still find Pembrokeshire's past without too much effort.

Above: Pontfaen Chapel is the most imposing building in secretive Cwm Gwaun

Right: Fishguard Fort on Castle Point, built in 1781, still mounts a battery of original nine-pounder cannon

4 Land use, culture and customs

The forces of nature are seen as the real creators of the Pembrokeshire landscape ...

Brian John, *Pembrokeshire Past and Present*, 1996

Above: The wide view from the 1,000ft summit of Mynydd Dinas encompasses the strange hills around St David's
Opposite top: A secluded meadow in autumnal Cwm Gwaun
Opposite below: Kingcups beside the river in early May: Clyn Wood, Cwm Gwaun

Humans have been altering and adding to Pembrokeshire's landscape for over 5,000 years, yet despite this the natural landscape stands proud of all Man's works.

Pembrokeshire was one of the main areas of Neolithic settlement in Wales, when the natural appearance of the area began to change as people cleared the great forests that had developed after the Ice Age in order to provide grazing areas for sheep and cattle.

As the populations of people and animals increased and technology improved through the Bronze and Iron Ages, the forest clearances continued, and the first field systems were also created. Some of these 2,000-year-old field walls can still be seen below the summit of Carn Llidi near St David's, and there are similar traces on Skomer Island.

By 1000AD only about 20 per cent of the area was tree-covered, as opposed to some 80 per cent after the Ice Age, and tree clearance and the development of grazing and crop lands continued to be the dominant influence on Pembrokeshire's landscape through to the twentieth century. In the Dark Ages, the

Laws of Hywel Dda and *The Mabinogion* both refer to the loss of woodland, while in 1603, George Owen wrote: '... this country groaneth ...with the decreasing of woods, for I find by matter of record that divers great cornfields were in times past great forest and wood'.

At the turn of the twentieth century, only 5 per cent of Pembrokeshire remained tree covered. The area's woodlands had disappeared over the centuries to make space for agricultural land or had been felled for charcoal burning, building and ship construction, coal mining (for pit props) and numerous other uses. The situation was not helped by two World Wars, which further depleted local woodlands, and today no visitor to the area can fail to notice the general lack of tree cover.

Currently woodland covers approximately 6 per cent (some 8,650 acres or 3,500ha) of the National Park, with the Gwaun, Nevern and Daugleddau valleys the largest wooded areas. Historically important are Pengelli Forest and Tŷ Canol Wood on the lower slopes of the Preseli Hills, both of which are National Nature Reserves and provide some idea of what the natural landscape of the area would have looked like before deforestation took place. Tŷ Canol is also nationally important for its 370-plus species of lichens.

As woodland declined, agriculture expanded, and from the Neolithic on there are few areas other than coastal headlands and uplands that have not been farmed. Pastoral farming has tended to dominate except

COED CYMRU

It is only in the last decade or so that opportunities for conserving and enhancing woodland quality and creating new woodlands have developed significantly through the Forestry Authority's Woodland Grant Scheme and the work of Coed Cymru, both in partnership with the National Park Authority.

on the coastal fringes, where potatoes and cereals are grown. Pembrokeshire is renowned for its early new potatoes, a particularly important crop for many farmers. Dairy farming has long been the dominant feature of the livestock economy except on the Preseli Hills, which are obviously more suited to sheep farming. Cattle and sheep were driven to market in England along drovers' roads, some of which still exist today.

Although Pembrokeshire has generally escaped the worst ravages of large-scale intensive farming, modern agriculture has had some negative effects on the landscape. These include post-war intensification of grassland management, conversion of marginal land into grassland, large, intrusive modern farm buildings and neglect or environmentally unsympathetic management of features, such as farm woodland, coastal slopes and traditional field boundaries.

With the introduction of EU policies encouraging schemes such as farm diversification and environmentally friendly farming (reduced use of fertilisers and maintenance of traditional field boundaries, for example), and the launch in 1999 of the Wales-wide Tir Gofal (Care for the Land) scheme run by the Countryside Council for Wales (CCW), there are now opportunities for farmers and the National Park Authority to work together to manage, conserve and protect the landscape.

Opposite: Sheep scamper across Rhos Fach Common, below Carn Menyn, Preseli Hills
Below: Summer meadow near Pisgah on the Cresswell River, Daugleddau

HEDGES AND BANKS

Hedgerows and stone/earth banks are a feature of the Pembrokeshire landscape which have generally fared better than in many other parts of the UK, and they provide good wildlife habitats and corridors for wildlife movement.

Opposite: The Texaco oil refinery at Rhoscrowther is seen at dusk from Wallaston Cross
Below: All that remains of an old sailing barge on the tidal Carew River near Lawrenny Quay

In recent years the National Park Authority has also worked closely with bodies such as the National Trust and the Wildlife Trust West Wales to develop environmentally friendly farm and land-management schemes.

Many traditional farming practices actually help wildlife. For example, sheep and cattle grazing on coastal slopes produce a good habitat for the chough. And on the fringe of upland areas agriculture has generally proved unproductive, allowing wildlife habitats to survive, while some marginal areas such as wetlands and lowland heath have also survived for the same reason. Pembrokeshire's wetlands have largely been drained, but examples do still occur at Penally Marsh (SSSI) near Tenby and at Castlemartin Corse, while good examples of lowland heaths can be found at Dowrog Common (SSSI) near St David's, on the lower slopes of the Preselis and in the coastal area to the west of Goodwick. All these are important wildlife and plant habitats.

The marine and coastal environment is an equally important feature of the National Park. The major use of the shoreline up until the twentieth century was for the development of harbours serving fishing and trading vessels. Many ports and harbours which appear quiet today were once heaving with activity – examples include the various settlements along the Daugleddau from which coal was exported in the nineteenth century; Milford Haven, the sixth largest fishing port in Britain in the early twentieth century, and Porthgain, where over 100 vessels were registered a century ago.

Today the main activity of the National Park's harbours is restricted to catering

for a limited number of local fishing boats, visiting sailors and the ever-increasing numbers of tourists. This means providing facilities for those visitors, all of which can put pressure on the environment and local resources.

Overcrowding is also becoming an issue. In summer, traffic jams are common along the narrow roads and lanes of places likes such as St David's, Tenby and Dale; popular beaches such as Saundersfoot and Whitesands can border on over-crowded (both in and out of the water), and heavily used sections of the Coast Path can suffer erosion from the impact of thousands of walkers' boots.

Some sections of the coast may be badly eroded by wind and wave action, and sea defences such as the groynes at Amroth may be required in order to minimise this. With the predicted rise in sea level and possible intensification of winter storms as a result of global warming, this problem may get worse in the future.

A further contentious issue is the siting of the various oil refineries and Pembroke Power Station (due for demolition at the time of writing) within the Milford Haven waterway, on the fringes of the National Park. Apart from the obvious visual intrusion of these developments, which can be seen from many areas, the environmental impact is also a major concern. The worst-case scenario came about in February 1996 when the oil tanker *Sea Empress* ran aground just inside the Haven and released some 72,000 tonnes of crude oil into the waters both inside the Haven and off Pembrokeshire's south coast. Around 124 miles (200km) of coastline were affected and several thousand birds died, and had the wind not been predominantly offshore during the event, the impact would have been far worse.

MILITARY RANGES

Seemingly out of place within a National Park are the various military training areas, primarily Castlemartin, Penally and Manorbier. These were in existence before the National Park came into being, and while they restrict access to some of the finest stretches of coastline within the Park, they have actually been of benefit to wildlife. Apparently the whizz and bang of military hardware doesn't bother the ranges' resident animals and plants, and many rare species are to be found on the Castlemartin Range because the land has remained uncultivated for over fifty years. (For access times to Castlemartin Range see the local press or ask at information centres or Bosherston Post Office.)

CULTURE AND CUSTOMS

I wish I could give you some idea of the exultant strangeness
of this place.

Graham Sutherland, 1942

The term 'Land of Mystery and Enchantment' may sound like a twee phrase dreamt up by an advertising agency, but as a description of Pembrokeshire it actually dates back to at least the twelfth century, and in terms of both culture and customs it sums up the area almost as well now as it did then.

Even a thousand years ago Pembrokeshire had a rich cultural legacy. The various standing stones and remains which dot the landscape from the Neolithic, Bronze and Iron Ages can't fail to have exercised the imaginations of later generations, as is apparent in tales from *The Mabinogion*. In the story of the lovers Culhwch and Olwen, for example, King Arthur and his knights pursue the monstrous great boar Twrch Trwyth from Ireland across the Irish Sea to Porth Clais near St David's. From there the chase took them up into the Preseli Hills, where the boar slays some of Arthur's knights and turns them to stone at the rocky outcrop called Cerrigmarchogion, which means 'the rocks of the knights'.

Further east along the ridge of the Preselis is Beddarthur, the grave of King Arthur (although it must be said that Arthur has several graves in south-west Britain), and the whole of the Preseli area has associations with the distant past. Other examples include Bedd Morris standing stone above the Gwaun Valley, which is said to commemorate a young man who was killed in a duel for the hand of a local girl, whilst on Carningli, above Newport, St Brynach is said to have communed with the angels (although bear in mind the profusion of magic mushrooms hereabouts!).

Many myths surround Pembrokeshire's numerous saints. St David came into the world in dramatic fashion, born to his mother St Non during an elemental storm which abated at his birth, at the same time as a spring issued forth at what is now St Non's Bay. Here you'll find a thirteenth-century chapel dedicated to St Non along with an incomplete circle of standing stones – an interesting fusion of pagan and Christian tradition.

At Whitesands, St Patrick is said to have embarked for Ireland to eventually become, like St David in Wales, the country's patron saint, and in the south the mysterious St Govan has been linked to King Arthur as Sir Gawaine. In an equally mythic but alternative role, as an ascetic and holy man St Govan is said to have sheltered from enemies at the spot where his chapel now stands after

Opposite: Autumn dawn on Cerrig Lladron: eastwards rises Foel Cwmcerwyn, the highest point of the Preseli
Below: St Non's Chapel stands on the cliff top close to St David's

LEGEND OF ST GOVAN

The story is that if you enter the cleft where St Govan sheltered and wish before turning round to come out, your wish will be granted. Water from the holy well below the chapel was once said to cure eye ailments and rheumatism, and earth from fissures around the chapel used to be sprinkled around homes to avert evil. Try counting the steps up and down to St Govan's Chapel – the number is supposedly always different going down to going up.

the rocks split to allow him to enter, then closed again. After his enemies had gone the rock opened and St Govan stepped out, supposedly leaving the impression of his body on the rock.

These myths and legends don't stop at the water's edge, either. The Cantref y Gwaelod, or 'Bottom Hundred', was said to be a great tract of fertile land extending from Ramsey Island to Bardsey Island at the northern end of Cardigan Bay. It had towns and cultivated land, and was defended from the sea by a strong embankment and sluices. The Keeper of the Embankment was Seithennin, said to be 'one of the three immortal drunkards of Britain', and one night, while living up to his name at a great banquet, he left the sluices open and the land was flooded. It's said that when the waters of Cardigan Bay are very still and clear you can see the walls and buildings of Cantref y Gwaelod, and the church bells may sound faintly.

There were also supposed to be islands out at sea other than those we see today, on which lived the Tylwyth Teg, or Fair Folk – basically, fairies – who sold their produce at local markets.

Less mythical but just as romantic are heroic tales from the Middle Ages. The future Henry VII's march from Mill Bay near Dale to do battle with Richard III at Bosworth Field in 1485 has already been mentioned, but there are interesting tales associated with Henry's arrival in Pembrokeshire. On landing, Henry consulted a local bard and prophet, Dafydd Llwyd, to find out how he would fare in his forth-

Above: Carew Castle looks down over its moat - the tidal Carew River

coming battle. Dafydd was doubtful about the success of the mission, but on his wife's advice told Henry that he would fare well, for as she wisely pointed out, if Dafydd was wrong Henry would be in no position to do anything about it, and if Henry won, Dafydd may make his fortune.

Henry's arrival also placed Sir Rhys ap Tudor of Carew in a quandary, for although Henry offered him the post of Lieutenant of all Wales in return for his support, he had given his oath to Richard III that anyone wishing to challenge the crown would have to do so 'over his belly'. He got around this by lying beneath Mullock Bridge near Dale as Henry crossed it, thus allowing himself to join Henry with his own band of 5,000 men for the march to Bosworth.

Sir Rhys was made a Knight of the Garter by Henry in 1497, and ten years later finally got around to celebrating this with the last great medieval tournament in Britain held at Carew Castle from 21 to 25 May, 1507. The highest-ranking noblemen in Wales and their ladies were invited, and 500 of the ablest men competed in a huge tournament which included tilting, throwing the bar, tossing the pike and wrestling.

The sea has been a part of everyday life for many Pembrokeshire residents over the centuries. Before the arrival of the railways, the sea was one of the main arteries for travellers coming to or from Pembrokeshire. Until the twentieth century, shipwrecks were a regular feature of life along the Pembrokeshire coast, known for

PROFIT FROM DISASTER

Local people often benefited from disasters at sea. Whisky Galore scenarios were not that uncommon – in fact whisky was exactly the cargo that came ashore at Angle when the Loch Shiel *was wrecked in 1894 - and there are more grisly accounts of people hacking fingers off drowned mariners to steal their rings. The residents of Llanunwas, near Solva, had a reputation in the eighteenth century for hanging out false lights to decoy ships into running aground.*

its treacherous rocks and currents. George Owen in the sixteenth century described how the Bishops and Clerks rocks west of Ramsey: 'preache deadly doctrine to their winter audience, such poor seafaring men as are forcyd thether by tempest'.

Arguably, the worst storm ever to hit the area was in October 1859. It destroyed St Brynach's church at Cwm-yr-Eglwys, threw up the pebble bank at Newgale and wrecked 114 ships off the Welsh coast.

In order to reduce such risks, the first lighthouse off the Pembrokeshire coast was erected in 1839 on South Bishop Rock, and the first lifeboat introduced to the area in 1869. Since then, the local RNLI crews have logged up a brave and illustrious history. In one tragic case, the St David's lifeboat *Gem* sank and lost three of its crew while attempting a rescue in 1910.

The Pembrokeshire coast was the setting for the last invasion of Britain in 1797. A motley assortment of convicts and ne'er-do-wells making up a French force under the command of the Irish-American General Tate came ashore at Carregwastad Point near Strumble Head, and enjoyed a few days pillaging in the local countryside before, as legend has it, they capitulated to the local militia. The heroine of the event was forty-seven-year-old cobbler Jemima Nicholas, who single-handedly captured fourteen French soldiers.

Close to Fishguard you'll also find one of Pembrokeshire's more unusual

Opposite: As it approaches Ramsey Sound the Coast Path passes the tidal islets of Cerreg Fran and Cerreg yr Esgob
Below: The ruined church of St Brynach at Cwm-yr-Eglwys on the shore of Newport Bay was destroyed in the great storm of October 1859

ST DAVID'S DAY

A major cultural event is the celebration of St David's Day on 1 March, when adults wear a Tenby daffodil in their lapel at the very least, and primary school children wear the national dress for the day. This is obviously a day of particular importance in St David's.

customs. In the Gwaun Valley (Cwm Gwaun) New Year's Day is celebrated on 13 January. This dates back to 1752, when the Julian calendar was replaced by the Gregorian calendar in the rest of Britain. In Cwm Gwaun, however, *Hen Galan*, or the Old New Year, is still celebrated by local families. Of course, the residents of Cwm Gwaun also make the most of 1 January too!

Another tradition that lives on is that of *cnapan*, a fourteenth-century game similar to rugby which was played in Newport until very recently. And, of course, there is the most famous Welsh tradition of all, the National Eisteddfod, and the venue for this huge cultural event in 2002 is St David's.

Usually, however, it's smaller events that bring colour to everyday life, such as town and village carnivals each summer (however small, few settlements don't hold one), and the three-day County Show in Haverfordwest each August. Smaller towns like Nevern also have their fairs, and there are low-profile local horticultural shows, sheep dog trials and dog and pony shows throughout the summer.

Coastal communities such as Solva and Little Haven have their annual regattas, and those towns with lifeboat crews will hold lifeboat days, which may feature a launch of the lifeboat. There are regular summer races up and down the coast between Pembrokeshire longboat crews, while surf lifesaving clubs from Pembrokeshire and sometimes the rest of Britain frequently compete against each other on local beaches.

Details of these events can usually be found in the National Park's free visitor newspaper *Coast to Coast*.

LITERARY AND ARTISTIC CONNECTIONS

Pembrokeshire features strongly in *The Mabinogion*, a classic collection of myths and folk tales dating back to the tenth and eleventh centuries. Not long after *The Mabinogion* was written, Giraldus Cambrensis of Manorbier wrote *The Itinerary through Wales* (1188), which provides some fascinating historical insights into life in twelfth-century Wales.

In 1603, George Owen of Henllys, near Nevern, published *The Description of Pembrokeshire*, which is still in print today. It provides a detailed account of everyday life in Elizabethan Pembrokeshire – Owen even goes so far as to tell readers the length of Pembrokeshire's longest and shortest days (17 hours 43 minutes and 6 hours 17 minutes respectively according to his calculations) along with a wealth of other information.

Two hundred years later, Richard Fenton of St David's published his *Historical Tour of Pembrokeshire*, a surprisingly easy and sometimes amusing read (for instance Fenton derides the myth that the St Govan's steps cannot be counted, stating categorically that he totted up fifty-two on his visit), while in 1888 Edward Laws, a gentleman scholar, published the phenomenally detailed *History of Little England Beyond Wales*.

More accessible to modern readers are the books of R.M. Lockley. This famous naturalist's work includes *Pembrokeshire* (1957), *In Praise of Islands* (1957), and *The Island* (1969), and not only look at the wildlife and landscape of the area but also describe Pembrokeshire life in the mid-twentieth century. The books of local author Roscoe Howells (including *The Sounds Between* [1968] and *Farewell the Islands* [1977]) are set in a Pembrokeshire which in many ways is rapidly becoming a thing of the past. Welsh-language poet Waldo Williams, writing in the first half of the twentieth century, also captured the essence of Pembrokeshire's landscape, and his work is now available in English translation.

Opposite: Cottages at Llanwdna above Carregwastad Point

Writers who have passed through the area and made brief comment include Norman Lewis (*The World, The World*), Paul Theroux (*The Kingdom by the Sea*) and Jan Morris in her partisan and passionate book *The Matter of Wales*.

A local author worth checking out whilst you're in the area is Brian John of Newport, whose work includes walking guides, histories and folk-tale collections. One of the best for an overall view of Pembrokeshire is *Pembrokeshire Past and Present*.

However, it's artists rather than writers for which Pembrokeshire is best known. The clarity of the light and the spectacular landscapes have been attracting painters to the area for at least 200 years. J.M.W. Turner painted at Carew, and

Tenby was the home of Augustus and Gwen John and Nina Hamnett in the early twentieth century. The work of all three can be seen in Tenby Art Gallery (in the museum), along with studies of Caldey Island by Eric Gill and David Jones.

But perhaps the best-known of Pembrokeshire's artists is Graham Sutherland who moved here for, among other things, the quality of light which he found 'magical and transforming'. At the time of writing, his collection, which has been bequeathed to the county, has no permanent home.

Artists and craftspeople are still drawn to Pembrokeshire for inspiration, and as you travel around the National Park you should take time to call in at a gallery or craft shop and take a look at the results of that inspiration.

Below: Caldey Island rides the horizon beyond Lydstep Point in this view south-eastwards from the cliff top above Skrinkle Haven

5 Recreation

Reading through some of the earlier publications about the Pembrokeshire Coast National Park, a visitor could be forgiven for thinking there was little to do here other than look at wildlife and flowers, visit the islands, and walk the Coast Path. Even as late as 1991 the official guide to the National Park managed to avoid any specific mention of recreational activities other than walking, although the public had been out there enjoying themselves on land and water for decades.

Although it took some time for the Authority to fully realise the richness and variety of the recreational resources within the Park, it is now working quite successfully to ensure that people can enjoy these resources while having a minimal impact on the natural environment and other people. Perhaps the best example of this is the Pembrokeshire Outdoor Charter, developed by local outdoor centres and other organisations working closely with the National Park Authority, the CCW and the National Trust, and aimed at encouraging appropriate sporting activities within the Park.

Pembrokeshire can probably offer more variety of recreational activities than any other National Park in the country - it's even occasionally possible to ski and snowboard in the Preseli Hills. Many activities are organised by the National Park Authority through their Activities and Events programme, including guided walks, cycle rides, horse rides and boat trips – full details are available in their free newspaper *Coast to Coast*.

What follows is a brief run-down on the most popular outdoor activities practiced in the National Park.

WALKING

The famed Pembrokeshire Coast Path, a 186-mile (299km) National Trail, took seventeen years of access negotiation and development before being officially opened by Wynford Vaughan Thomas on 16 May 1970. The majority of the Coast Path crosses privately owned land, and in the few places where the path takes a detour inland (such as the Castlemartin Artillery Range) you can generally assume that access isn't permitted – often, as in this example, for good reasons.

The path runs from Amroth in the south to St Dogmael's in the north, and can be walked fairly comfortably in two weeks. Along its length you'll tramp along, beside and above some of the finest coastal scenery in Europe.

Some areas, such as the Whitesands to St David's Head section, are often very busy due to a combination of easy access, good walking, and inspiring views, yet if you're seeking solitude you often need do little more than continue for a mile or two past the 'honeypot' areas and you'll soon be striding along the cliff top alone.

WALKING ON THE PRESELIS

Inland you'll also find exhilarating walking across the Preseli Hills, which rise to 1,759ft (536m) at Foel Cymcerwyn, the highest point in Pembrokeshire. On a clear day you can see most of west Wales from here, and sometimes even the Wicklow Hills in Ireland.

Opposite: A rock climber in action on Saddle Head on the Range East section of the Castlemartin coast: perfect limestone high over the sea

CLIMBING CONSERVATION

The climbing community has long worked with the National Park Authority and other conservation organisations to ensure that the important colonies of cliff-nesting birds are not disturbed as a result of climbing. Restrictions on Range East in south Pembrokeshire have also been agreed with the MOD, although occasional protests against restricted access have been know to take place here in the past.

The more popular sections of the Coast Path have to withstand a great deal of wear and tear, although erosion from walkers' boots is not yet a major problem, and continued maintenance by the National Park Authority and the National Trust has ensured that busier areas don't get worn out - and quieter sections of the path don't become overgrown.

Although a low-level route, some sections of the path are quite challenging and it's best to be just as well equipped for a full day out on the Coast Path as you would be for a day walking in the hills.

Three walks which capture the essence of the Pembrokeshire Coast Path are the previously mentioned Whitesands to St David's Head route (but take a detour up 593ft [181m] Carn Llidi for tremendous views); a tramp along the spectacular sea cliffs at Castlemartin (when the Army isn't firing), perhaps with a detour to Bosherston Lily Ponds; and the walk out along the Dale Peninsula, where you can enjoy magnificent views of Skomer, Skokholm and the various smaller islands.

Below the Preseli Hills in the Gwaun and Nevern valleys there is fine and generally easy walking through woodlands and beside rivers and streams, where you may just spot otters and herons. Back towards the coast, the inland waters of the Daugleddau Estuary also have relaxed easy walking in quiet surroundings, where often the only sound is the water lapping against the banks and the wind soughing through the trees.

There are also a number of paths in the Park with disabled access, including routes at Haroldston Chins in St Brides Bay, at Stackpole Estate in south Pembrokeshire and between Pwllgwaelod and Cwm-yr-Eglwys near Dinas. More details on these are available from the National Park Authority and information centres.

CLIMBING

There are two distinct areas of sea-cliff climbing – the exposed limestone sea cliffs of the Castlemartin area, and the gabbro and dolerite cliffs of the north coast, specifically the areas around St Bride's Bay, St David's Head and north towards Strumble Head. Both areas provide an excellent range of routes from easy scrambles for beginners to extreme routes for experts.

Since all these locations combine superb coastal scenery and a wealth of marine and terrestrial wildlife habitats, it's no exaggeration to say that Pembrokeshire has some of the finest sea-cliff climbing in Europe.

The sport in the north of the county was largely pioneered in the 1960s, since when climbers from all over Britain have continued to visit and put up more and ever harder routes. Suzie's Plot on Rainbow Zawn, for instance, is recognised as one of the finest extreme climbs in Wales. One of the great attractions of the north coast is its solitude. On a warm summer's day there are few experiences in climbing to match being on the rock face as the sun beats down, seabirds glide and wheel above your head and porpoises or grey seals can be seen in the water below.

South Pembrokeshire's cliffs were first scaled as early as 1929-30 at Giltar Point, but it wasn't really until the late sixties that the area began to be opened up by Colin Mortlock (also responsible for 'discovering' north Pembrokeshire), Lyn Noble and Jim Perrin. The sea cliffs here can provide excellent climbing to suit all standards, and being south-facing, in warm, sunny conditions it's possible to climb in shorts and T-shirt, even – sometimes – in winter.

To be sure you're not climbing 'out of season' check for notices at climbing locations or contact the National Park Authority for their access leaflet.

Above: A clean, late summer swell provides perfect surf conditions (John Isaacs)

QUEUING TO SURF?

In the mid-nineties the National Park Authority was among a number of groups and organisations which helped to put together a free advisory leaflet aimed at avoiding crowd problems in the surf at Whitesands, one of the worst affected beaches. This was probably a first for the UK, but despite this overcrowding continues to be a problem in the waves at many beaches.

SURFING

One of Pembrokeshire's major attractions for surfers is the opportunity to surf in clear green waters surrounded by beautiful scenery.

The south of the county tends to have the most consistent waves, and Freshwater West is regarded as one of the best surf beaches in Wales. Other popular spots in south Pembrokeshire include Broad Haven South, Manorbier, Freshwater East and Tenby South Beach, although the latter two are generally only winter breaks.

North Pembrokeshire's best-known surf beach is Whitesands, a rather overrated beach which has nevertheless been popular for over thirty years. Newgale Sands is another favourite, particularly with beginners, while at the opposite end of the scale the black sands of Abereiddi can often provide more challenging waves. In winter, as with the south of the county, many more breaks such as Broad Haven and Abermawr start to work thanks to the big winter swells that swing in from the Atlantic.

Overcrowding can be a serious problem in surfing, where the unwritten rule is that the first surfer to catch the wave should have it exclusively to themselves – which can lead to lots of frustration when thirty or more people are all trying to surf the same break.

This is not something that is going to go away as surfing continues to increase in popularity, and the solutions are not obvious. Perhaps artificial reefs would be one way forward for surfing in the twenty-first century?

SAILING

Pembrokeshire's offshore waters can provide some of the finest and most challenging sailing in Britain. Experienced sailors will find that the prevailing south-westerlies, which blow year-round and can vary from a gentle breeze to a gale, can take them on unforgettable voyages along the coast and around the islands. Although it takes skill and experience to negotiate the many tidal streams that result from the meeting of the waters of the Irish Sea and St George's Channel, particularly in spots such as Ramsey Sound and Jack Sound off Skomer, the rewards are great. Not only is there a wealth of seabirds to view, but the waters are home to everything from Atlantic grey seals to porpoises, dolphins, basking sharks and occasionally even whales, all of which can be seen far better in open waters than from any headland or island.

The anchorages within the National Park vary from small, hidden harbours such as Solva and Angle, to the clamour and colour of Tenby or Saundersfoot, and just outside the National Park there are good marinas at Neyland and Milford Haven.

More sheltered waters can be found in the Milford Haven waterway and the Daugleddau Estuary. This spectacular inland waterway has unfortunately been marred by the industrial developments towards the mouth of the estuary. However, once you sail under the Cleddau Bridge and head up either the Eastern or Western Cleddau this disappears from view, and it's easy to relax and enjoy the pastoral landscape on either side of the river, maybe stopping off at one of the small villages such as Cresswell Quay, Lawrenny Quay or Llangwm. As the tide drops you'll also notice a wide range of wildfowl and waders feeding on the mudflats and sandbanks.

Below: Running down Ramsey Sound off the southern end of the island - with the outlying Ynys Cantwr on the left

DIVING

The area's crystal-clear waters provide some of the finest diving conditions in Britain, with the added bonus of the warming influence of the Gulf Stream, particularly in summer. There are numerous wrecks on which to dive, with slipways from which to launch dive boats at many locations. One of the most popular is Little Haven, where there is excellent access to the Marine Nature Reserve off the coast of Skomer Island. Whitesands is also a popular launching site with divers.

Experience and tuition are vital before you head off into the open waters off the Pembrokeshire coast, and it's also important to have first-hand knowledge of the often powerful tidal stream and currents which flow around many popular dive sites. Because of the importance of the marine habitats, particularly that around Skomer, a Diving Code of Practice has been produced by the National Park and the Skomer Marine Nature Reserve, which is recommended reading before heading out to sea.

WINDSURFING

The boom years for windsurfing (excuse the pun) in Pembrokeshire were the eighties, since when interest in the sport has tailed off somewhat. This may be in part due to the capricious wind and sea conditions for sailing off many of the beaches, which means that for anyone other than experienced sailors it can be tricky making the most of the Pembrokeshire coastline.

However, skilled windsurfers will find that wide, open beaches such as Tenby South Beach, Broad Haven, Newgale, Whitesands and Newport Sands allow you to get up plenty of speed, and strong winds are often accompanied by swells which allow for good wave-jumping conditions.

Less experienced sailors will find some fine sheltered waters as well as being able to enjoy the above beaches on calmer conditions. For virtually guaranteed flat water, Dale Roads inside the Milford Haven waterway is excellent, and has been the venue for several national and international windsurfing events.

FISHING

The stretch of coastline between Druidston and Freshwater West is generally regarded as one of the finest sea-fishing areas in Wales, largely due to the wide variety of fish available.

The beach casting can be excellent – a wide variety of fish can be caught including sea bass, and spinning for mackerel, bass and pollock is popular from the rocks. A world record tope (74lb) was once caught in Saundersfoot, although this has since been bettered.

Estuary fishing may also be rewarding, with good catches of bass and flounder possible in the Teifi estuary around Poppit Sands and in the creeks of the Milford Haven waterway.

The National Park's rivers can provide good bags of salmon, sewin (sea trout) and brown trout. The number of fish running the rivers increases from August onwards, and after dark the fly fishing can be excellent. Worth checking are the rivers Nevern and Taf, on the eastern edge of the Park. The River Gwaun, surrounded by beautiful woodlands, is in private hands, but local landowners may give permission to fish here.

Right: View northwards along the wide beach of Freshwater West, a favourite surfing venue, towards the sand dunes of Broomhill Burrows and the southern cliffs of the Angle Peninsula

Please remember to take all your tackle home with you – wildlife, birds in particular, can easily become entangled in discarded lines and hooks, and some areas of the coastline can become a real mess in summer due to thoughtless anglers.

CYCLING AND MOUNTAIN BIKING

Cycling and mountain biking are two of the fastest-growing family activities in Pembrokeshire. There are a number of marked cycle trails, especially in south Pembrokeshire, but even without using these you'll find that cycling is an easy and rewarding way to discover the area for yourself. Villages and hamlets, secluded coves and hidden standing stones can easily be reached on a bike, and I'd say I've discovered as much of Pembrokeshire on my bike as I ever have on foot or through reading guide books.

The mountain biking in the National Park is limited – and the Coast Path, being a *footpath* for the most part, is out of bounds – but there are some good routes around the Preseli Hills and the Gwaun Valley, and various mix-and-match routes of bridleways and roads along the coast both north and south of the Milford Haven waterway and along the Daugleddau.

Committed off-road riders really need to look to the Preseli Hills for their action and check carefully that they're riding on legally accessible routes (also note in wet conditions the riding here is often heavy going). Depending on your route you can stop off at sites such as Pentre Ifan, Carn Menyn (one of the sources of the bluestones of Stonehenge) and Castell Henllys Iron Age village.

All it takes is a map and a little time to put together your own route for discovering the National Park by bike.

CANOEING AND KAYAKING

Pembrokeshire has some of the finest sea kayaking in Europe, whilst the Daugleddau Estuary and the Milford Haven waterway are excellent waters for both kayaking and canoeing.

Areas of coastline which are inaccessible to any other form of craft can be reached by sea kayak, including the offshore islands. The low environmental impact of this activity makes it probably the best way to explore the Pembrokeshire

HORSE RIDING AND PONY TREKKING

Discovering Pembrokeshire on horseback allows you to see a great deal more than you can by any other means of transport, simply because of the extra height you've gained.

Many of the bridleways and tracks on which you can ride have been used for millennia, perhaps, for instance, as old drovers' roads, along which flocks of sheep and cattle would have been driven to market in England. Some have linked together settlements since the Bronze Age, a good example being the Golden Road along the ridge of the Preseli Hills, which dates back over 3,000 years. Riding in these hills is one of the best ways to see Pembrokeshire as you can look down across the whole of the National Park and beyond.

Horses have been an important part of life in Pembrokeshire since Celtic times, as can be seen from a trip to the remains of Carnalw Iron Age fort in the Preseli Hills, which is defended by a chevaux de frise, a ring of sharp, upright stones thought to be placed to stop attacks on horseback.

Back down on the coast it's also possible to ride on some beaches. Galloping through the surf on a sunny morning is guaranteed to get your senses buzzing.

Left: Mountain biking through Pen-yr-allt Wood

coastline and see at close hand the seabird colonies, seals, porpoises and other marine mammals. It's possible to make trips along the coast and out to the islands that last from a morning to several days.

For adrenalin junkies, The Bitches rapids in Ramsey Sound provide some extremely challenging kayaking and have been used in the past for world championship events. Surf kayaking is popular at many of the more open beaches, although as with surfing overcrowding can be a problem.

Travelling by canoe or kayak allows you to get very close to wildlife in its natural environment, but at the same time care should be taken not to cause any undue disturbance.

SEA BATHING

Bathing in the sea is one of the oldest recreational activities in the National Park, and still one of the most popular for three main reasons – great beaches, relatively warm seas in summer and some of the cleanest waters in Britain. Many beaches have won environmental awards as denoted by the flags flying above them in summer – blue indicates the highest standard EC Blue Flag award, and pale blue and yellow is the Tidy Britain Group award.

On a hot summer day there will be few beaches in Pembrokeshire where someone isn't taking a dip, from quieter corners like Porth Melgan, Traeth Llyfn and Watwick Bay to such well-known spots as Newport, Whitesands, Broad Haven and Tenby (which, incidentally, saw its first bathers in their bathing carriages in the nineteenth century).

The more popular beaches have lifeguards in summer, but for many people the fact that you can still find relatively quiet beaches, even at the height of the holiday season, is a big attraction. However, if you're swimming from an isolated beach you should watch out for any rips and currents.

With the increasing popularity and availability of wetsuits, bathing – as with all the other watersports practised in Pembrokeshire – is now potentially a year-round activity. Of course, some people don't believe in this new-fangled gadgetry, so every New Year's Day you'll find a bunch of enthusiasts in Tenby, at Whitesands

PADDLING YOUR OWN CANOE
Paddling in an open Canadian canoe alongside the steep wooded river banks and gently sloping farmland of the upper Daugleddau is a rewarding and relaxing experience. There are numerous little 'pills' and creeks to explore, and much of the area is internationally important for its wader and wildfowl populations.

Opposite: Sea kayakers emerge from exploring a deep cave in the cliffs at Porth Dwgan, Aberbach
Left: Evening on Newport Sands, with Dinas Head on the horizon

and doubtless at other beaches up and down the National Park, who insist on taking their dip in nothing more than swimming trunks or bathing costumes – and sometimes not even that!

BOATING

All the major islands can be visited (although not always landed on) by regular pleasure boats or more powerful jet boats.

You can circumnavigate or land on Ramsey, Skomer, Skokholm and Caldey, though you can only circumnavigate Grassholm and its huge gannet colony. A boat trip also gives you the opportunity to see Pembrokeshire's mainland from an entirely different angle. Trips are available from various spots including Tenby, Solva, Whitesands Bay and Porthgain.

Boat trips often also focus on wildlife activity, such as viewing puffins in early summer, offshore rafts of Manx shearwater in high summer, or watching the new seal pups in autumn. Or they may be for nothing more than sheer fun, such as blasting by jet boat through the roaring waters of Ramsey Sound. There is obviously an element of disturbance to wildlife from motorised boat trips, but operators by and large are well aware of the impact both they and their customers may have and do their best to keep it to a minimum.

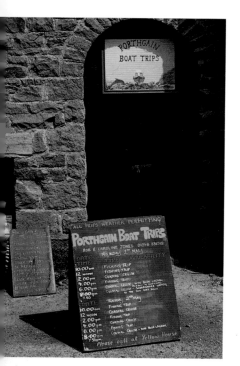

Above: Local boatman's board at the little harbour of Porthgain
Right: A boatload of visitors on passage from Skomer to the mainland at Martin's Haven
Opposite: A coasteering party in action below the cliffs near Aberbach

COASTEERING

Coasteering developed in the nineties in Pembrokeshire. It involves traversing sea cliffs just above sea level in a wetsuit, trainers, buoyancy aid and safety helmet, and features climbing, scrambling, cliff-jumping, swimming and quite a bit of falling into the sea.

With the current craze for adrenalin sports, anyone who has tried coasteering once will understand its popularity, and Pembrokeshire's craggy coastline is perfectly suited to the sport. Research has shown its impact to be minimal if sites are chosen carefully, and it can actually provide people with a view of the harsh intertidal world that they would never otherwise see.

With all these activities on offer it's little surprise that the Pembrokeshire Coast National Park is becoming an increasingly popular destination for outdoor enthusiasts, and this trend shows every sign of continuing to grow.

6 Exploring the Park

AMROTH

Amroth marks the beginning and end of the 186-mile (299km) Pembrokeshire Coast Path, and sits on the Carmarthenshire border. It was a mining village when the local area was worked for coal and iron. The numerous groynes, acting as sea defences, are an indication of the village's constant battle with the sea. On very low tides you may see a submerged forest here, the remnants of an ancient forest dating from about 5000BC.

BROAD HAVEN

A popular resort with locals and visitors since the early twentieth century, Broad Haven is the largest beach town in north Pembrokeshire. The town has a number of shops

and pubs and an excellent sandy beach, some great coastal walking nearby, and impressive geological features in the cliffs at either end of the beach.

There is a National Park Information Agency in the youth hostel next to the town's main car park, and there are also a number of camping and caravan sites in the vicinity.

CALDEY (YNYS PYR)

Caldey Island, which lies 2 miles (3km) south of Tenby, was first settled in the sixth century by Celtic monks. In 1136 it was granted to the Benedictine Abbey of St Dogmaels who founded a priory here, which was dissolved by Henry VIII in 1536. After this the islanders farmed and quarried limestone until Caldey was again bought by a Benedictine monastic order in 1906 and sold on in 1929 to the Cistercian Order, which in 1958 raised the monastery to build an abbey. Boats leave Tenby daily for the island in the summer, where attractions include a perfume shop selling herbal fragrances distilled by the monks.

CAREW (CAERIW)

The main attractions here are the castle and Celtic cross, although Carew's location beside the Carew River is pleasant enough. Carew Castle is an excellent example of the development of a castle from Norman times (although as a defensive site it is

Opposite: A view over Broad Haven at the outflow of the Bosherston lily pools; not to be confused with the resort of the same name on St Bride's Bay

Below: There is excellent rock climbing on the steep limestone cliffs of Lydstep Point, which display spectacular folds and other geological features. Caldey in the distance

Above: The little village of Dale lies near the mouth of Milford Haven. In this view across Dale Roads the evening sun lights Musselwick Point beyond
Opposite above: Low tide in the Gwaun Estuary - the sheltered harbour of Fishguard Lower Town. This, the original Fishguard harbour, has been the setting for various films

believed to date back to the Iron Age) through to an Elizabethan fortified manor. The name of the village may be a corruption of the Welsh *caerau* (fort).

The present castle was developed in the twelfth century by Sir Nicholas de Carew as a rectangular fortress with turrets at each corner. This was enhanced by Sir Rhys ap Thomas around 1500, while the North Range with its impressive Elizabethan façade was added by Sir John Perrot of Haroldston, Lord Deputy of Ireland and said to be the illegitimate son of Henry VIII.

The castle and the nearby Carew French Mill, first mentioned in records in 1542 and the only still-intact tidal mill in Wales, are leased to the National Park Authority and are open to the public. There are walks around the castle and mill, including disabled access. Also worth checking out at Carew is the finely inscribed and sculpted Celtic cross, erected in memory of Mareddud, the ruler of Deheubarth (west Wales), who was slain in 1035.

DALE

Dale was a smuggler's village in the Tudor period, and today is popular with sailors and windsurfers. The village and local roads can become very congested in summer.

At nearby Mill Bay, Henry Tudor (later Henry VII) landed on 7 August, 1485, prior to gathering his armies and marching to Bosworth Field where he defeated Richard III to take the crown of England.

FISHGUARD (ABERGWAUN)

Fishguard and its satellite of Goodwick (Wdig) are ringed by the National Park boundary. Fishguard was a Viking settlement (*Fisgard*, or 'fish yard'), and today is best known as the terminal for the Irish Sea ferry service (which is actually in Goodwick).

The town sits on a headland with excellent views over the Irish Sea, while Lower Town, down a steep hill just east of the main town, is a picturesque little harbour. It was the location for the 1971 film of Dylan Thomas' *Under Milk Wood*.

The Royal Oak Inn in the centre of Fishguard was the scene for the surrender of the French invasion force in 1797. The heroine of the event, Jemima Nicholas,

is buried in St Mary's churchyard, next to the Royal Oak. In St Mary's Church Hall there's a tapestry depicting the events of the invasion, created to mark its 200th anniversary.

Fishguard Harbour was built in 1906 as a port for transatlantic passenger liners. However, the vessels built for this service eventually became too big to use the port.

There are Tourist Information Offices in Goodwick's Ocean Lab building and in Fishguard, and the Irish Sea ferry leaves from Fishguard Harbour for Rosslare.

Below: The tiny church of St Brynoch at Pontfaen in Cwm Gwaun is one of the smallest in Britain and contains some beautiful medieval murals

GWAUN VALLEY (CWM GWAUN)

There are two 'major' settlements in the Gwaun Valley, the hamlets of Llanychaer and Pontfaen. Llanychaer is a small cluster of houses and a pub, with close by the church and 'cursing' well of the lost settlement of Llanllawer, which is reputed to have provided curses and ill omens in return for a bent pin. To the east of the church is Parc y Meirw (Field of the Dead), seven standing stones which make up the longest megalithic alignment in Wales.

At Pontfaen there is the beautifully restored St Brynach's Church which has two stone crosses dating from the sixth-ninth centuries and an intricate interior. A visit to the Dyffryn Arms pub here is a real trip back in time.

HAVERFORDWEST (HWLFORDD)

Pembrokeshire's county town and the headquarters of the National Park Authority and local government is not actually in the National Park. Some interesting architecture is unfortunately lost among a selection of modern shop fronts and an uninspired riverside shopping centre.

Haverfordwest developed around its castle, built around 1120 by Gilbert de Clare. The oldest remaining features are thirteenth century, and the ruins (the castle had fallen into disuse by 1520) overlook the town from a steep hill. Tumbling down from the castle are narrow streets of medieval origin which feature some attractive buildings dating from the seventeenth, eighteenth and nineteenth centuries, when the town prospered as a port lying at the tidal limit of the Western Cleddau.

Down by the river warehouses and quays can still be seen alongside the Bristol Trader Inn. Shipping died off with the arrival of the South Wales Railway in 1853.

St Mary's Church is the most interesting of Haverfordwest's three churches, dating back to the thirteenth century. The lower part of the town is the main shopping area. The district museum is next to the castle, and there is a small National Park Information Centre in the High Street, while the main TIC is by the bus station.

LAWRENNY

Lawrenny is an attractive village of well-restored cottages just inland of the Cresswell River and the Daugleddau. It is dominated by the four-storey tower of twelfth-century St Caradoc's church. Lawrenny Quay was once important for river-borne exports and imports and is now popular with sailors. A track runs from the church up to the site of the old castle, from which there are superb views across to the confluence of the Cresswell and Carew rivers with the Daugleddau. The walk along the river bank through ancient oak woodland, with views across the river to Benton Castle, is well worth while.

LITTLE HAVEN

Little Haven is a picturesque village at the southern end of St Bride's Bay. From the sheltered, shingly little beach, backed by pubs, the village's cottages twist and

Below: The rocks of Black Mixen below Lawrenny Hill divide the confluence of the Cresswell and Carew rivers before they join the Daugleddau

wind their way back inland and up the hillside. Little Haven was once a centre of the local coal-mining industry, with coal being exported from the beach, but now it is a popular spot with swimmers and divers, who launch their boats there.

At low tide the walk along the beach to Broad Haven is excellent – look out for the interesting geology and caves of the sea cliffs.

MANORBIER

In the twelfth century Giraldus Cambrensis (Gerald of Wales) famously described Manorbier as 'the most delectable spot in Wales', and even today you can see what he meant. The village and its castle and church stand above the attractive Manorbier Bay and look out across some fine coastal scenery.

The castle was built and added to in the twelfth and thirteenth centuries by members of Gerald's family, the de Barris, and Gerald was born here c1146. The castle is open to the public from April-September, and highlights include the coastal views from the ramparts and exploring the dark passageways of the walls and buildings.

The parish church on the opposite side of the valley also dates back to the twelfth century, although it was rebuilt in the fourteenth. The beach is very popular with bathers and surfers, and a short walk south on the Coast Path leads to the King's Quoit, a Neolithic cromlech.

Above: The ramparts of Manorbier Castle rear over the narrow valley. The castle is still a private residence
Below: This is the tidal lagoon at the head of Dale Roads, an inlet of Milford Haven. Beyond rises the Gann

MILFORD HAVEN (ABERDAUGLEDDAU)

Although Milford Haven's name is of Norse origin, the town was founded in the late eighteenth century by a group of Quakers from Nantucket who had left their

home due to the American War of Independence. They developed the town's grid-work of streets, but the docks were not completed until the mid-nineteenth century.

Despite being located on one of the finest natural harbours in the world, Milford Haven never really achieved success as a port and harbour. A shipbuilding contract with the Admiralty in the early nineteenth century was lost to Pembroke Dock, and the docks never managed to attract ocean-going liners, although Milford did become a major fishing port for a time and in 1906 it was the sixth largest fishing port in Britain.

During both World Wars the harbour and town were busy dealing with Atlantic convoys, but after World War II the fishing industry declined rapidly and now only a handful of mostly foreign-owned trawlers use the harbour.

The nearby refineries have brought work to the area at the expense of the landscape, and recently a series of tourist attractions have opened in the new marina.

The town museum is worth a visit, and Fort Hubberston, west of the town, is an unusual Palmerston defence fort built in the 1860s which you can explore.

If you can ignore the refineries, many of which are no longer operating, the views across the Haven's waters from the town's pleasant gardens are impressive.

NARBERTH (ARBERTH)

Narberth is a friendly, busy little town in the heart of the quiet, rural landscape of the Landsker Borderland. The town can trace its origins back to the days of *The Mabinogion*, a collection of ancient Welsh folk tales. Narberth was supposedly the site of the court of Pwll, and the ruined twelfth-century castle – in much its present state by 1590 – was indeed the home of Welsh princes.

The unusual Town Hall in High Street was built in the 1830s and hides the municipal water tank beneath. In recent years Narberth has taken on the role of the 'capital' of the Landsker Borderlands – you can find out more about the area in the Landsker Visitor Centre, alongside the TIC in the town hall.

The Wilson Museum in Market Square is worth a visit to see a collection made up largely from items donated by local people.

NEYLAND

Neyland, on the Milford Haven waterway, has a busy marina with all the associated facilities, and sits close to the impressive Cleddau Bridge. The town was originally known as New Milford, and developed after being selected by the famous Victorian engineer Isambard Kingdom Brunel as the site of the terminal for the projected South Wales to Manchester railway. Neyland further developed as the terminal for the Irish Packet Service until the Irish Sea ferry service was transferred to Fishguard in 1906, and was for a time an important deep-sea fishing port. There are way-marked walks and a cycle trail around the surrounding area.

NEVERN (NANHYFER)

Once the administrative and religious centre of the area, Nevern is best known for its church, St Brynach's. One of the ancient yews in the churchyard is know as the 'bleeding yew' because of the brown-red sap which oozes from its bark. In the windows of the south transept are two inscribed stones, the possibly fifth-century Magloconus Stone, with Latin and ogham inscriptions, and the Cross Stone, which features an early Celtic cross. Outside the church is Nevern Cross, a superb tenth-century Celtic cross. On a bluff above the village sits what little is left of the ruined thirteenth century Nevern Castle.

NEWPORT (TREFDRAETH)

This pleasant little town lies above the broad sweep of Newport Bay, and continues a centuries-old tradition of electing a mayor, a legacy of the time when it was the chief settlement of the local Norman Marcher Lordship of Cemaes. Every May, the mayor, Lord Marcher and local MP carry out the tradition of 'Beating the Bounds', when they literally beat out the town's bounds as well as small boys at Bedd Morris standing stone above the town, apparently to encourage the boys to remember Newport's boundaries! Court Leets are still held in the town, and the Norman castle (an 'utter ruin' by the sixteenth century but restored in 1859) looks down from above the settlement.

The local beach is well worth a visit, and there are some fine walks on the local coast and hills. The Newport Eco Centre in Lower St Mary Street has free exhibitions on sustainable living. There is a National Park Information Centre in Long Street.

PEMBROKE (PENFRO)

Pembroke's main attraction is its magnificent castle, although the fine Museum of the Home and attractive main street of Georgian and Victorian houses are also worth a look. The castle was built shortly after the Norman conquest in the late eleventh century, then almost entirely rebuilt between 1189 and 1245. For the following three centuries it was used as an important tool by the English in establishing firm military rule throughout the area (the Welsh, despite numerous attempts, never gained control of Pembroke Castle).

The earldom of Pembroke, created in 1138, was granted along with the castle

Above: The little town of Newport and its castle look down on the pretty harbour at the mouth of the Afon Nyfer

to Jasper Tudor in 1452 by Henry VI. Jasper's nephew Harri (or Henry) was born here in 1457 and later went on to become King of England after defeating Richard III at Bosworth Field in 1485.

During the Civil War Pembroke Castle was sacked by Cromwell after the town's military governor switched allegiance from the Parliamentarians to the Royalists. Centuries of subsequent neglect led to the castle becoming derelict, although over the last 120 years it has been substantially restored. What remains is still a superb monument to the past, particularly the huge Norman keep which is 75ft (23m) high and has walls 18ft (5.5m) thick, and the castle is well worth a visit whether you're a history buff or not. There is a TIC on The Commons.

PEMBROKE DOCK (DOC PENFRO)

Built in the nineteenth century on a grid pattern, Pembroke Dock was developed as an Admiralty Dockyard in 1814 and continued thus until 1926. Some 240 ships were built here, including in 1852 the *Duke of Wellington*, the largest ever three-deck man-of-war, and all the Royal Yachts, apart from the last *Britannia*. The old dockyard was a flying-boat base during World War II, and in recent years the nearby oil refineries have brought work at a cost to the landscape.

The town has some handsome Victorian buildings, and the Gun Tower (a converted Victorian military defence post) on Front Street is a museum and TIC of some interest, but most visitors today tend to be passing through on their way to or from the town's Irish ferry service.

PORTHGAIN

Porthgain oozes atmosphere. Its little harbour is still in use, and the industrial past of the village is very obvious in the disused brick works, red brick hoppers (above the harbour) and nearby slate and stone quarries. The attractive little cottages around the village green were built for workers, and Tŷ Mawr, the large building in the centre of the village was a centre of much of this activity. Inside the excellent Sloop Inn you'll find some fascinating photos and mementoes of the village's past. This is a fine place to visit for a short coastal walk and an alfresco pint on a summer's evening.

Above: This 'Palmerston Folly' Gun Tower beside the old dockyard wall is one of several incorrectly dubbed 'Martello Towers', and was built in 1851 to defend Pembroke Dock against the French
Right: Granite and slate quarried close by were once shipped to London and elsewhere from the tiny harbour of Porthgain

ROSEBUSH

Rosebush developed as its quarries grew in the 1870s. There was a railway to transport the slate, and a short-lived tourist industry also developed at the same time, much of this thanks to the entrepreneur Edward Cropper. Remnants of the slate industry are obvious (Rosebush slates were used to roof the Houses of Parliament), and the tourist industry was centred around the unusual and interesting Tafarn Sinc pub, once a hotel, which had associated ponds and ornamental gardens.

Rosebush is a good base for walking, pony trekking or mountain biking in the Preseli Hills.

ST DAVIDS (TY DDEWI)

What is essentially a small and fascinating village was granted official city status by the Queen in 1995. The famous cathedral is situated in the hollow of the Alun Valley, and St David is said to have been born at nearby St Non's Bay, where there is a chapel and well dedicated to his mother, Non. According to tradition, David founded the cathedral in AD550, although construction of the present building was begun by Bishop Peter de Leia in 1180. Even before this St David's was an important ecclesiastical centre, attracting pilgrims from all parts of Britain, including William the Conqueror.

Clichéd as it sounds, if you visit St David's you really *have* to visit the cathedral. Highlights include the intricate latticed oak roof; the elaborate fourteenth-century rood screen; the unique monarch's stall, reserved for the Queen (the only such stall in Britain); and Bishop Vaughan's chapel with its beautiful sixteenth-century fan tracery roof.

Across the river from the cathedral are the evocative ruins of the Bishop's Palace, which dates from around 1340 and was built to house the bishop of St David's and his staff. It was in ruins by the sixteenth century.

Up in the 'city centre' is a Celtic cross dating from the fifteenth century, from

THE CULT OF ST DAVID

St David - the sixth-century Welsh bishop - became Dewi Sant, the patron saint of Wales. In medieval times the St David's peninsula, the land beyond the Western Cleddau, was known as Dewisland to the pilgrims who flocked there to visit his shrine. Many came by sea from Cornwall, Ireland, North Wales or even Brittany, landing at Porth Clais where the monks built a breakwater, and making the short journey to the shrine via St Non's Holy Well and Chapel, and nearby Whitewell Chapel. Others came on foot from the north via Strata Florida and Nevern, or from the east via Whitland Abbey, Llawhaden and Treffgarn, on routes well defined by lesser shrines and pilgrim hospices, and which are still possible to follow.

Once elaborately decorated, and missed somehow by the destructive zeal of the Reformation, something of St David's shrine still exists between the two stone pillars on the north side of the cathedral presbytery. His actual relics are believed to rest in an oak and iron casket still displayed in a stone niche behind the high altar.

Opposite & pages 103–4: Porth Clais harbour in its sheltered inlet close to St David's

which the generally pleasant main streets fan out, and there is a new, purpose-built National Park Visitor Centre on the main St David's–Haverfordwest road.

The surrounding coastline and countryside provide everything from superb walking to swimming, surfing and climbing, and although always crowded in summer St David's is one of the most memorable spots in Pembrokeshire.

SAUNDERSFOOT

Saundersfoot developed around its harbour, built to export high-quality anthracite from the local coalfield via the narrow-gauge Saundersfoot Railway. The industry was at its peak in the nineteenth century, with the last colliery closing in 1939.

Today Saundersfoot is a busy and popular holiday resort, with the harbour being full of pleasure craft and the local beaches among the most popular in Pembrokeshire.

SOLVA (SOLFACH)

One of the most picturesque settlements in the National Park, Solva is popular with sailors, and the harbour and Lower Town are always busy in summer. A few locally owned fishing boats operate out of the harbour but most are pleasure craft, although in the early 1880s over thirty vessels used to trade from here.

On The Gribin, the headland on the south side of the harbour, are the remains of Iron Age earthworks. There are superb views from here, and the small beach you can see to the south was the site on which the first lighthouse for The Smalls was built in 1773. It was shipped out to sea from here, and then was erected on the outermost rocks.

Above: Colourful cottages line the main street of Solva village at the head of the harbour

TENBY (DINBYCH-Y-PYSGOD)

The fascinating town of Tenby has a rich history, much of which is revealed through its buildings. The most immediately obvious features when entering Tenby are the town walls, built in the thirteenth century and strengthened in 1457 by Jasper Tudor, Earl of Pembroke, then again in the 1580s against possible attack by the Spanish Armada. Five Arches is the most impressive feature of the walls and is the only town gate to survive.

Fifteenth-century St Mary's Church and its elegant 152ft (46m) spire is the centrepiece of the town, and other buildings worth seeing include the Tudor Merchant's House on Quay Hill, which has a fine Flemish chimney and was built in the late fifteenth century when Tenby was second only to Bristol as a west coast port; Laston House (1810-11), a former sea water baths which bears the Greek inscription meaning 'the sea washes away the ills of men', and the remains of the Norman castle on Castle Hill.

The attractive harbour shelters fishing boats, pleasure craft and the Caldey Island ferry boats, and is backed by a fine selection of Georgian and Victorian town houses. Beside the harbour is North Beach, often crowded but convenient for the town, while to the south, around the headland and past St Catherine's Island with its Victorian defensive fort, is South Beach and its long stretch of golden sands.

A Town Trail which provides full details of Tenby's rich architectural history is available from the TIC on The Croft.

Tenby was Pembrokeshire's first seaside resort, with people travelling to take the waters here from the early nineteenth century, and it is still one of the most popular holiday resorts in south Wales.

Above: 'Five Arches', the medieval south gate barbican (top) on the ancient town walls, pierced also by the Belmont Arch (above) linking St Florence Parade to the Paragon

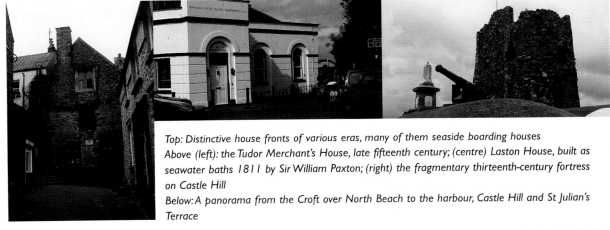

Top: Distinctive house fronts of various eras, many of them seaside boarding houses
Above (left): the Tudor Merchant's House, late fifteenth century; (centre) Laston House, built as seawater baths 1811 by Sir William Paxton; (right) the fragmentary thirteenth-century fortress on Castle Hill
Below: A panorama from the Croft over North Beach to the harbour, Castle Hill and St Julian's Terrace

Information

USEFUL ADDRESSES

Pembrokeshire Coast National Park
   Authority
Winch Lane
Haverfordwest
Pembrokeshire SA61 1PY
Tel: 01437 764636

National Trust – Wales
Trinity Square
Llandudno
LL30 2DE
Tel: 01492 860123

National Park Visitor Centres

Newport Information Centre
Bank Cottages
Long Street
Newport
Tel: 01239 820912 (seasonal)

St David's Information Centre
The Grove
High Street
St David's
Tel: 01437 7203392

Other Bodies

CADW (Welsh Historic
   Monuments)
Brunel House
2 Fitzalan Road
Cardiff CF2 1UY
Tel: 029 2050 0200

Council for the Protection of Rural
   Wales
Ty Gwyn
31 High Street
Welshpool
Powys SY21 7YD
Tel: 01938 552525

Countryside Council for Wales
Plas Penrhos
Ffordd Penrhos
Bangor
Gwynedd LL57 2LQ
Tel: 01248 370444

Wales Tourist Board
Brunel House
2 Fitzalan Road
Cardiff CF2 1UY
Tel: 029 2047 5322

Wildlife Trust West Wales
7 Market Street
Haverfordwest
Pembrokeshire
SA61 1NF
Tel: 01437 765462

Attractions

Blackpool Mill and Caverns
Canaston Bridge
Tel: 01437 541233

Carew Castle and Tidal Mill
Carew
Tel: 01646 651782

Castell Henllys Iron Age Fort
Newport
Tel: 01239 820912

Lamphey Bishop's Palace
Nr Pembroke
Tel: 01646 672224

Manorbier Castle
Manorbier
Tel: 01834 871394

Milford Marina
Milford Haven
Tel: 01646 696300

Museum of the Home
7 Westgate Hill
Pembroke
Tel: 01646 681200

Pembroke Castle
Main Street
Pembroke
Tel: 01646 681510

Picton Castle
Near Haverfordwest
Tel: 01437 751326

St David's Cathedral
St David's
Tel: 01437 720199

*Left: Tenby: the elegant Regency
houses of St Julian's Terrace look
down on the harbour in this view
from the Mayor's Slip*

St David's Bishop's Palace
St David's
Tel: 01437 720517

Tenby Museum and Art Gallery
Castle Hill
Tenby
Tel: 01834 842809

The Tudor Merchant's House
Quay Hill
Tenby
Tel: 01834 842279

West Wales Eco Centre
Lower St Mary Street
Newport
Tel: 01239 820235

Island Trips

Caldey
Coastal and Island Cruises
Tenby Harbour
Tenby
Tel: 01834 843545

Ramsey
Thousand Island Expeditions
Cross Square
St David's
Tel: 0800 163621

Skomer, Skokholm, Grassholm
Dale Sailing company
Brunel Quay
Neyland
Tel: 01646 601636

MAPS

The use of the excellent range of Ordnance Survey maps is highly recommended for any detailed exploration of the Park.

Outdoor Leisure Maps (1:25,000)
No 35: North Pembrokeshire
No 36: South Pembrokeshire

Landrangers (1:50,000)
No 145: Cardigan & surrounding area
No 157: St David's & Haverfordwest area
No 158: Tenby & surrounding area

FURTHER READING

Delaney, F. *The Celts* (Harper Collins, 1993)

Donovan, J., and Rees, G. *Birds of Pembrokeshire* (Dyfed Wildlife Trust/Nature Conservation Bureau Ltd, 1994)

Fenna, J. *Heritage Walks in Pembrokeshire* (Sigma Leisure, 1997)

Gantz, G. (trans) *The Mabinogion* (Penguin, 1976)

Gerald of Wales. *The Journey Through Wales/The Description of Wales* (Penguin, 1978)

Goddard, T. *Pembrokeshire Shipwrecks* (Hughes, 1983)

Howells, R. *Farewell the Islands* (Gomer Press, 1987)

John, B. *Pembrokeshire Coast Path (National Trail Guide)* (Aurum, 1997)

— *Pembrokeshire Past and Present* (Greencroft Books, 1995)

— *Pembrokeshire 2000, Land and People* (Greencroft Books, 1999)

— *The Last Dragon – A Book of Pembrokeshire Folk Tales* (Greencroft Books, 1992)

John, T. *Sacred Stones* (Gomer, 1994)

Marine Conservation Society. *The Reader's Digest Good Beach Guide* (updated annually) (David & Charles)

Miles, D. *A Pembrokeshire Anthology* (Hughes, 1983)

Owen, G. *The Description of Pembrokeshire* (Gomer, 1994)

Rees, S. *Dyfed: CADW Guide to Ancient and Historic Wales* (HMSO, 1992)

Saunders, D. (editor), *The Nature of West Wales* (Barracuda, 1986)

Index

Page numbers in *italics* indicate illustrations